T0194341

WINDOWS TO THE WORD

RHONDA K. KINDIG

WESTBOW
PRESS®
A DIVISION OF THOMAS NELSON
& ZONDERVAN

WestBow Press books may be ordered through booksellers or by contacting:

WestBow Press
A Division of Thomas Nelson & Zondervan
1663 Liberty Drive
Bloomington, IN 47403
www.westbowpress.com
1 (866) 928-1240

ISBN: 978-1-9736-6364-5 (sc)
ISBN: 978-1-9736-6365-2 (e)

Library of Congress Control Number: 2019906504

Print information available on the last page.

WestBow Press rev. date: 06/04/2019

Contents

Preface

From the first chapter in John's Gospel, when Jesus asks, "What are you looking for?", folks are trying to figure out who Jesus is. Evangelist John charts the responses as people who encounter Jesus draw their own conclusions. Jesus describes himself in John's Gospel by using seven great metaphors. Do these sound familiar?

"**I am** the *bread of life*." (John 6:35)

"**I am** the *light of the world*." (John 8:12)

"**I am** the *gate for the sheep*." (John 10:7)

"**I am** the *good shepherd*." (John 10:11)

"**I am** the *resurrection and the life*." (John 11:25)

"**I am** the *way, the truth, and the life*." (John 14:6)

"**I am** the *vine*." (John 15:5)

Each one of the metaphors offers a glimpse into the mystery of Jesus. By digging deeper into the Bible, we can uncover greater understanding about each of these symbols. Let's open the windows of scripture to discover the layers of meaning in each of these images, or icons.

Purpose

Have you ever noticed that particular words, such as "light" or "bread", seem to recur throughout the Old and New Testaments? As one becomes more and more familiar with the Bible, certain concepts seem to echo from book to book.

The purpose of this book is to explore some of the myriad Biblical references that parallel the seven well-known metaphors for Jesus from the gospel of John, the "I am the" . . . bread/light/gate/shepherd/life/truth/vine sayings, to discover how they work as descriptions for Jesus and help us understand the mystery of who he is.

These symbols might also be called "icons" (which is the Greek word for "image"). Author Madeleine L'Engle believed that an icon is a window to God. Lots of everyday things became icons for her, as they reflected the wonder of God. [Madeleine L'Engle, <u>Penguins and Golden Calves</u>, Shaw Books, 2003]

Episcopal theologian Robert Farrar Capon wrote that icons are sacraments of the very real presence of the Word of God; he even calls them God's "fingerprints". [Robert Farrar Capon, <u>Fingerprints of God</u>, Eerdmans, 2000] Have you ever thought of God leaving fingerprints in the world?

Just how do these seven symbols from John interweave throughout scripture to illuminate our human understanding for the mystery of Jesus?

Preliminaries

A bit of background will be helpful, as we navigate between the Old and New Testaments of the Christian Bible. The Bible itself is a library of 66 books that were composed over millennia by multiple storytellers and authors. What Christians call the Old Testament is founded upon the Hebrew Bible, which the Jews call the "TANAKH". That name is an acronym for the three main parts that make up the Hebrew Bible:

TORAH (also called Pentateuch, the Law, or Books of Moses—tales of the patriarchs)

NEVI'IM (the scrolls of the prophets)

KETHUVIM (these are the "writings", such as Psalms, Proverbs, Ecclesiastes)

The contents of these books offer the narratives of the people of God as they experience God in their lives.

The Christian New Testament picks up the experiences beginning with the life and teachings of Jesus, delivered by very different voices and not necessarily eye witnesses. Each author has an audience and an agenda that shapes his text.

The New Testament opens with four gospel accounts of Jesus. The first three, Matthew, Mark, and Luke, are called *synoptic*, because they present Jesus with "the same eye"; the fourth, John, is *asynoptic*, because his approach, his chronology, and most of his content are unique. In addition, the New Testament contains various epistles, or letters, that have shaped Christian theology. The New Testament closes with Revelation, which is an unveiling of a multi-valent vision about Jesus.

Revelation is a word with a shocking synonym: Apocalypse. Modern folks who hear apocalypse often think of a final annihilation, but that is not the definition of this Greek word. No, apocalypse is an unveiling, a pulling back of the curtain, so you can look through the window! Lutheran theologian Barbara Rossing [Barbara Rossing, The Rapture Exposed, Westview Press, 2004] compares this to the tiny terrier Toto, in "The Wizard of Oz", pulling the curtain open to reveal the great and powerful Oz is not a wizard but an ordinary man.

Windows to the Word will be looking specifically at scriptural texts from John's Gospel, the source of the seven "I am the . . ." metaphors, and then commenting on parallels found in all three sections of the Hebrew Bible, as well as in the Gospels and book of Revelation from the New Testament.

Looking for parallels between Biblical narratives has been an illuminating exercise for scholars, dating back to the first church fathers in the early centuries after Jesus. Such study is called typology. That means that the Old Testament characters and events are "types" for the ones in the New Testament. It has been said that the New Testament is concealed in the Old Testament, while the Old Testament is revealed in the New Testament. Great reformer Martin Luther claimed that scripture should interpret scripture. This is most certainly true with the seven great metaphors in John!

Now a word about each metaphor's opener: "I am". For anyone having familiarity with the Hebrew Bible, this is loaded with meaning. Early in the Hebrew Bible, a man named Moses has an encounter with God in which God reveals himself to Moses.

Moses said to God, "If I come to the Israelites and say to them, 'The God of your ancestors has sent me to you,' and they ask me, 'What is his name?' what shall I say to them?" God said to Moses, "I AM WHO I AM." (Exodus 3:13-14)

This phrase in the original Hebrew actually expresses all tenses at once; other possible translations include: "I AM WHAT I AM" or "I WILL BE WHAT I WILL BE". A Greek translation would be "the existing one". In hymns and other references, you might hear God called, "The Great I AM".

The idea is that God is eternal, that God is living, that God is uncreated.

Of course, a name as holy as God's could never be pronounced by the people, so the Hebrew Bible will always substitute "LORD" (in all caps) to stand in place of the holy name.

Evangelist John fully expects his audience to recall "the Great I AM" when he shows Jesus speaking the seven great metaphors.

[For an explanation of literary terms, such as "metaphor", see Appendix Three.]

Primary Points about John

A comparison of the four evangelists will reveal that John is markedly different. It was written toward the very end of the first century AD/CE. (The Jewish Temple had been destroyed by Rome in 70 AD/CE, and we know John was written after that.) It is not an eye-witness account of Jesus. The author might have been named John, it might have been someone writing with the authority of John, or it might have been someone within a "community" of John. It was written to an audience of Jewish Christians who were struggling from being expelled from the Jewish synagogues because of their beliefs about a crucified and risen Messiah named Jesus.

With no Temple and no more access to synagogues, these Jewish Christians needed John's teachings to know how to reconcile their beliefs in this Messiah with their understandings about God and their worship of God.

What we find in John is quite unlike the synoptic gospels. Many beloved stories about Jesus are missing from John. John gives us no birth story, no baptism story, no temptation story, no exorcisms, no parables, no Sermon on the Mount, no Lord's Prayer, and even a different timetable for some important events.

John also gives us stories that are found in no other source: the wedding at Cana with water turned to wine; the raising of Lazarus from the dead; the foot-washing of the disciples; and extended conversations with people like Nicodemus and the Samaritan woman at the well, among others.

John is very systematic in following a year in Jesus' life, from one Passover feast to the following Passover, which turns out to be a New Passover: Jesus' own Passion story. Along the way, John relates his audience's understandings about God, from their ancient scriptural stories and rituals, to a new way of seeing these through the lens of a Risen Messiah named Jesus.

Some believe that John's Gospel is actually a catechism, wherein John seeks to transfer his readers' reliance upon Moses, as the mediator of God, to Jesus, as the human face of God. The seven "I Am the . . ." metaphors are an important part of this catechism.

The number seven is meaningful for John. Indeed, number symbolism is pervasive throughout the Bible. Seven, as in the seventh day of creation, represents completion. It is a perfect number. John deliberately provides seven (all we need!) great metaphors. He also has seven additional times when Jesus proclaims, "I am!" without a following metaphor. When that happens, Jewish authorities will think blasphemy, because they hear him claiming to be God.

[For more information about number symbolism, see Appendix Two.]

I am the bread of life.

John 6:35

What does scripture tell us about the bread of life?

<u>In the Torah</u>

Bread from Heaven

In the 17th chapter of Exodus, we read that the Israelite people, having been rescued from their slavery in Egypt by God, are grumbling that they do not have food they want in the Sinai wilderness. So, God institutes a "manna economy". Each weekday the Lord would rain down bread for the people to gather their daily sustenance. On the sixth day, a double portion was rained down, so there would be enough for the seventh day, the Sabbath day, on which no manna would be given. As holy time during Sabbath, the people were to focus solely on God that day, ceasing from all worldly activity.

The name "manna" actually means, "What is it?" The Exodus narrative tells us it was a fine, flaky substance, as white as frost. It could be prepared any way one wished—baked or boiled. It tasted pleasingly like honeyed wafers.

It was an "economy", because it taught the people to rely on God for their sustenance. Everyone got exactly the amount needed. There was no hunger. There was no want. There were no "have's & have not's". There was no exploitation. There was no hoarding, because manna would spoil by the next morning. There was no surplus. There was no lack.

The manna ceased on the day the people crossed over the Jordan River into the Promised Land of Canaan. However, a jar of manna was kept in the Holy of Holies beside the Ark of the Covenant in the Tabernacle and later the Temple as a remembrance.

"Remember the long way that the LORD your God has led you these forty years in the wilderness, in order to humble you, testing you to know what was in your heart, whether or not you would keep his commandments. He humbled you by letting you hunger then by feeding you with manna, with which neither you nor your ancestors were acquainted, in order to make you understand that one does not live by bread alone, but by every word that comes from the mouth of the LORD." (Deuteronomy 8:2-3)

Bread of Presence

In the latter chapters of Exodus, Moses is given instructions for building and furnishing the Tabernacle. This was a portable tent for the very presence of God to dwell among his people, wherever they went. In fact, the word "tabernacle" was a verb, as well; God would "tabernacle" with the people.

The inner sanctuary was furnished with very holy objects, including a table for the "Bread of the Presence". This was not ordinary bread. There were twelve loaves (for the twelve tribes of Israel), given as an offering to God each Sabbath, as a reminder of the everlasting covenant.

Bread of the Presence represented God's continued presence with the people. The literal translation for "Bread of Presence" is "Bread of the Face". The people were to see the bread as a visible sign of God's face.

On the pilgrim festival of Pentecost (celebrating the fiftieth day in the wilderness when the people were given the gift of the commandments), the priests would elevate the Bread of the Face before all the people and say, *"Behold God's love for you!"* [Brant Pitre, <u>Jesus and the Jewish Roots of the Eucharist</u>, Doubleday, 2011]

3

Bread of Promise

The prophets were the voice of the LORD, speaking words of exhortation and encouragement, especially before, during, and after their exile from their homeland. Prophetic messages were more about description than prescription (forth-telling rather than foretelling!).

One of John's purposes for writing his gospel was to show his readers that Jesus was fulfilling the Old Testament prophecies. As the "bread of heaven", Jesus, whom John names "The Word", provides everything needed for sustenance, as promised by the prophets.

For example, in Isaiah, the prophet encourages his listeners that God will restore them after their exile:

"For as the rain and the snow come down from heaven,
and do not return there until they have watered the earth making it bring forth and
sprout, giving seed to the sower and bread to the eater,
so shall my word be that goes out from my mouth;
it shall not return to me empty,
but it shall accomplish that which I purpose,
and succeed in the thing for which I sent it." (Isaiah 55:10-11)

In Ezekiel, for instance, the people are reminded of God's care for them through the gift of bread:

"My bread that I gave you—
I fed you with choice flour and oil and honey—
You set it before them as a pleasing odor;
And so it was, says the Lord GOD." (Ezekiel 16:19)

Bread of Plenty

The Hebrew Writings include liturgies, such as prayers and songs. There are lists of aphorisms and advice. There are moral tales. References to the gift of bread are sprinkled among the Writings.

"He rained down on them manna to eat,
And gave them the grain of heaven.
Mortals ate of the bread of angels;
He sent them food in abundance." (Psalm 78:24-25))

"I will abundantly bless its provisions;
I will satisfy its poor with bread." (Psalm 132:15)

"Open your eyes, and you will have plenty of bread." (Proverbs 20:13)

In the Gospels

Daily Bread

The prayer that Protestant Christians call "The Lord's Prayer" and Roman Catholics call "The Our Father" is introduced in both Matthew and Luke. Each has this petition:

"Give us this day our daily bread." (Matt 6:11; Luke 11:3)

Does this seem redundant to ask each "day" for "daily" bread? The Greek original reads a bit differently! The word shown as "daily" is, in fact, not from the Greek word for "daily". It is actually a word best translated as "supernatural"! What is meant by this? It most likely was meant to be "manna" or "bread from heaven", in the sense that Jesus taught.

Bread of Life

Three annual Jewish festivals were so important that every able-bodied adult male was required to make a pilgrimage to the Temple in Jerusalem to participate:

Pesah or Passover,
Shavuot, Festival of Weeks, or Pentecost, and
Sukkot or Festival of Tabernacles/Booths.

Passover remembered God's mighty act of deliverance from bondage in Egypt. Shavuot occurred fifty days later, commemorating the gift of the commandments. It coincided with the spring barley harvest. Sukkot was an autumn festival of ingathering.

John's Gospel opens Jesus' ministry, in chapter 2, near the time of Passover. In the 5th chapter, when Jesus goes to Jerusalem for a festival, it has to be Shavuot, during which offerings of grain were given, particularly the first barley of the season. Jesus next feeds a multitude from two loaves of *barley* bread in the 6th chapter of John.

The next day, Jesus speaks of the crowd's motivation for seeking him. He counsels them, *"Do not work for the food that perishes, but for the food that endures for eternal life, which the Son of Man will give you." (John 6:27)* The crowd asks for a sign and tells Jesus, *"Our ancestors ate manna in the wilderness; as it is written, 'He gave them bread from heaven to eat.'" (John 6:31)*

Jesus responds, *"Very truly, I tell you, it was not Moses who gave you the bread from heaven, but it is my Father who gives you the true bread from heaven. For the bread of God is that which* comes down from heaven and gives life to the world." (John 6:32-33)* [*Your Bibles will offer a footnote that says there is an alternate translation choice—*"who comes down"*!]

At that point Jesus declares, *"I am the bread of life. Whoever comes to me will never be hungry, and whoever believes in me will never be thirsty." (John 6:35)*

6

Those first-century Jewish Christians who were expelled from the synagogues would no longer be able to celebrate the Festival of Weeks with their fellow Jews, but they do have Jesus supplying sustenance beyond barley.

Bread Blessed, Broken, Given

The gospels close their narratives with their descriptions of the last week of Jesus' life, the week of his crucifixion then resurrection. We learn of his Last Supper with his disciples, a meal during which we hear: *"Then he took a loaf of bread, and when he had given thanks, he broke it and gave it to them, saying, 'This is my body, which is given for you. Do this in remembrance of me.'" (Luke 22:19)*

Bread of life, indeed! Bread now takes on the sacramental quality of feeding us every time we partake in Holy Communion, which follows the pattern of the Last Supper.

In Revelation

John of Patmos writes seven letters to seven churches. His hope is to offer them encouragement to "Keep the faith!" despite Roman persecution. The churches who stay faithful are given promises. In his letter to the church in Thyatira, the promise is of manna:

"Let everyone who has an ear listen to what the Spirit is saying to the churches. To everyone who conquers I will give some of the hidden manna." (Revelation 2:17)

Pondering

How does the bread of life metaphor enrich your understanding of God? Of Jesus?

Consciously note every item that provides you sustenance this day.

Determine to sustain another in some fashion this day.

I am the light of the world.

John 8:12

What does scripture tell us about the light of the world?

<u>In the Torah</u>

Created Light

For openers, *"In the beginning, God said, 'Let there be light. And there was light.'" (Genesis 1:3)*

God speaks creation into being, starting with light—the first great gift. Light separated from darkness. Good light. Daylight. Sunlight. Everything builds on that.

Uncreated Light

A tradition developed, especially seen in works of art, that a fundamental quality of God's nature is "uncreated light". This is in contrast to "created light", such as sunlight, candlelight, or even electric light. The uncreated light surrounding God was given the Greek name empyrean (from the root word *"pyr"*, which is fire). In art forms, this is shown as golden.

When human beings experienced the divine in theophanies, there was often some aspect of uncreated light associated with the vision. Moses had a theophany beside a burning bush that was not consumed (*Exodus 3:2*); Elijah had a theophany with a fiery chariot (*2 Kings 2:11*). God led the Israelites through the wilderness for forty years by means of a pillar of cloud by day and a pillar of fire by night. (*Exodus 13:21*)

The theophany described in the 19th chapter of Exodus is witnessed by all the Israelites at the foot of Mt Sinai. There was more than just uncreated light involved in that meeting, all their senses were touched.

"On the morning of the third day there was thunder and lightning, as well as a thick cloud on the mountain, and a blast of a trumpet so loud that all the people who were in the camp trembled. Moses brought the people out of the camp to meet God. They took their stand at the foot of the mountain. Now Mount Sinai was wrapped in smoke, because the LORD had descended upon it in fire; the smoke went up like the smoke of a kiln, while the whole mountain shook violently." (Exodus 19:16-17)

Did you notice when this took place? On the third day? There are more references to "on the third day" in the Old Testament than in the New. It is a literary sign to pay attention, because God is about to do something amazing!

Presence of Light

When the Tabernacle is constructed, specific instructions are given for an elaborate seven-branched gold lampstand, called the menorah, to be constructed according to God's plan. (*Exodus 25:31-40; 37:17-23*) The botanical embellishments on the lampstand are suggestive of a tree of life motif. Similar plans are followed to illuminate the Temple built by Solomon. The perpetual light is a reminder of the very presence of God.

Light vs Darkness

Light, in contrast to darkness, is an obvious comparison throughout the prophetic writings.

"The people who walked in darkness have seen a great light;
Those who lived in a land of deep darkness—
On them light has shined." (Isaiah 9:2)

Light is both metaphorical and literal.

"I will lead the blind by a road they do not know,
By paths they have not known I will guide them.
I will turn the darkness before them into light,
The rough places into level ground.
These are the things I will do,
And I will not forsake them." (Isaiah 42:16)

"Arise, shine; for your light has come,
And the glory of the LORD has risen upon you.
For darkness shall cover the earth,
And thick darkness the peoples;
But the LORD will arise upon you,
And his glory will appear over you.
Nations shall come to your light,
And kings to the brightness of your dawn." (Isaiah 60:1-3)

Illumination

The Writings abound with references to light. Light always represents goodness.

"The Lord is my light and my salvation;
Whom shall I fear?" (Psalm 27:1)

"Light dawns for the righteous,
And joy for the upright in heart." (Psalm 97:11)

"The LORD is God,
And he has given us light." (Psalm 118:27)

Of course, there is also the illumination of understanding:

"The unfolding of your words gives light;
It imparts understanding to the simple." (Psalm 119:130)

"For the commandment is a lamp and the teaching a light." (Proverbs 6:23)

Walking in righteousness, is considered walking in the light:

"But the path of the righteous is like the light of dawn,
Which shines brighter and brighter until full day.
The way of the wicked is like deep darkness;
They do not know what they stumble over." (Proverbs 4:18-19)

Signs of Light

The birth narrative of Jesus, as told in Luke, records shepherds in the fields by night being terrified as the *"glory of the Lord shone around them." (Luke 2:9)* The very different birth narrative of Jesus offered by Matthew includes the wise men following a shining star. *(Matthew 2:1-12)*

John's prologue omits a birth narrative for Jesus, but attests to the light: *"What has come into being in him was life, and the life was the light of all people. The light shines in the darkness, and the darkness did not overcome it." (John 1:4-5)* This opening of John's Gospel definitely recalls the opening of Genesis.

Part of the Sermon on the Mount in Matthew has Jesus tell the disciples, *"You are the light of the world. ...Let your light shine before others, so that they may see your good works and give glory to your Father in heaven." (Matthew 5:14;16)* Obviously, the light is to be shared!

The synoptic gospels tell of a theophany of uncreated light experienced by disciples Peter, John, and James, as they witness Jesus, changed before them with an appearance of "dazzling white", in a story we call the Transfiguration. *(Luke 9:28-36; Matthew 17:1-9; Mark 9:2-10)* The disciples are astonished to see Old Testament heroes, Moses and Elijah, standing with Jesus on that mountain-top. They also hear the voice of God identifying Jesus as his own son.

Festivals of Light

In John's Gospel, Jesus celebrates the Jewish Festival of Booths in chapter 7. Also called the Feast of Tabernacles, this was another of the three great festivals that required Temple worship of the men. There was an elaborate ceremony of water during this time, but there was also a ceremony of light. Four great menorahs were set in the center of the women's court of the Temple. The men celebrated by dancing beneath these all night long for seven nights, during which time the Levites sang Psalms 120-134. Legend claims that these menorahs were so big and so bright that their light was reflected in every courtyard of Jerusalem.

It was during this light-filled atmosphere that Jesus offers himself as a "replacement" for this ritual. He is the "light of the world". (*John 8:12*) Jewish wisdom tradition had always claimed the Torah, or the Law, was the light of the world! The Way of Jesus also illuminates:

"Whoever follows me will never walk in darkness but will have the light of life." (*John 8:12*)

In the 10th chapter of John, Jesus attended the Festival of Dedication in Jerusalem. That would be Hanukkah, a celebration not found in the Torah. Also called the Festival of Light, Hanukkah commemorates a miraculous victory of light lasting despite not having enough oil to keep it burning. Households today light candles in menorahs each of eight days during this festival.

From Darkness to Light

In Mark, when Jesus breathes his last at the crucifixion, the Temple curtain is torn in two. In Matthew and Luke, for the last three hours Jesus is on the cross, *"darkness came over the whole land."* (*Matthew 27:45*)

In John's narrative, after Jesus' crucifixion, Mary Magdalene is the first to approach the tomb. She does so *"early on the first day of the week, while it was still dark."* (*John 20:1*) John wants his audience to recognize it was literally and figuratively dark, because no one yet knows of the resurrection. But we know that light will soon shine, and Mary Magdalene, in the new morning light, will be the first to witness the Risen Lord and the first to spread this good news. (*John 20:18*)

In Revelation

Light plays a dominant role in the conclusion of Revelation, indeed, in the concluding chapters of the Bible. A new heaven and a new earth are described, as the holy city, the New Jerusalem comes down from heaven, from God, to be the home for mortals with God. This is the uncreated light of the very presence of God.

"And the city has no need of sun or moon to shine on it, for the glory of God is its light, and its lamp is the Lamb. The nations will walk by its light." (*Revelation 21:23-24*)

Pondering

How does the light of the world enrich your understanding of God? Of Jesus?

What particular illumination have you perceived recently?

Consider how you might shine onto the life of another.

I am the gate for the sheep.

John 10:7

What does scripture tell us about the gate for the sheep?

Before we address the gate image, we must recognize that we are the sheep! The Israelite people in the Old Testament are predominantly herding tribes, so nothing could be more natural than images of sheep. Similes of the people as sheep are found regularly in the Old Testament:

"We are his people, the sheep of his pasture." (Psalm 100:3)

"I have gone astray like a lost sheep." (Psalm 119:176)

"All we like sheep have gone astray." (Isaiah 53:6)

"My people have been lost sheep." (Jeremiah 50:6)

"My sheep were scattered." (Ezekiel 34:6)

We will spend more time with the sheep in the next chapter, when we talk about the shepherd. Now for the image of gates. . .

<u>In the Torah</u>

Closed and Guarded

Although it is not specifically a gate, the first instance of a decided closure to a location occurs after the apple incident in Genesis, when the man and the woman are expelled from God's paradise for disobedience.

"He drove out the man; and at the east of the garden of Eden he placed the cherubim, and a sword flaming and turning to guard the way to the tree of life." (Genesis 3:24)

More secure than any gate, this guarded passage ends the previously known way of existence for Adam and Eve. Otherwise, gates are pretty straightforward in scripture and in life.

The great thing about gates is that they operate as metaphors in two opposite ways. Open, they offer invitation; closed, they offer protection.

<u>In the Nevi'im</u>

Temple Vision

The most symbolic reference to gates occurs in Ezekiel's Temple Vision, from chapters 40 through 48. There are upward of 75 mentions of the word gate, as the Temple is described and measured, with great emphasis on God returning to this Temple and the tribes of Israel having access through their own gates.

Symbolically, a gate allows easy access for God to return to the Temple. Then, these gates offer both invitation and protection, for the people of God, because the name of this New Jerusalem is *"God Is There"*. (*Ezekiel 48:35*)

<u>In the Kethuvin</u>

Temple Gates

The Psalms sing of access to the Lord through gates:

"Enter his gates with thanksgiving,
and his courts with praise." (Psalm 100:4)

"Open to me the gates of righteousness,
That I may enter through them
And give thanks to the LORD.
This is the gate of the LORD:
The righteousness shall enter through it." (Psalm 118:19-20)

Pearly Gates

As mentioned before, John of Patmos ends his Revelation with a glorious vision of a new heaven and new earth. The New Jerusalem, a holy city, comes down from heaven to become the home of God and mortals together. It is measured and described, as was the Temple Vision in Ezekiel, in symbolic numbers of perfection.

The foundations of the city are *"adorned with every jewel"*, while the *"twelve gates are twelve pearls, each of the gates is a single pearl, and the street of the city is pure gold." (Revelation 21:19,21)*

The number twelve is to suggest both the twelve tribes of Israel and the twelve disciples of Jesus, but access to the city is through an open invitation:

"The Spirit and the bride say, 'Come.'
And let everyone who hears say, 'Come.'
And let anyone who is thirsty come.
Let anyone who wishes take the water of life as a gift." (Revelation 22:17)

Pondering

Had you considered the dual role of gates before…as open invitations and as closed protection?

Has God opened a gate for you today?

Have you shut or opened doors to others in your journey this week?

I am the
good shepherd.

John 10:11

What does scripture tell us about the good shepherd?

Perhaps the most beloved image of Jesus and undoubtedly the most widely memorized verse in the Bible would be *"The Lord is my shepherd." (Psalm 23:1)*

As we saw in the previous section, with people so readily identified as sheep in scripture, it makes sense that the Lord would be the shepherd. We will find many such references in the Old and New Testaments.

In the Torah

God, the Shepherd

In the concluding chapters of Genesis, patriarch Jacob (by now called Israel) pronounces a deathbed blessing on his sons. He calls upon God as his shepherd when doing this, the first instance of God being identified this way:

"The God before whom my ancestors Abraham and Isaac walked, the God who has been my shepherd all my life to this day." (Genesis 48:15)

The twelve sons are assembled, and each in turn receives a blessing. Son Joseph, who saved his family, and a nation, from a severe famine, hears this from his father:

"Joseph is a fruitful bough, a fruitful bough by a spring; his branches run over the wall. The archers fiercely attacked him; they shot at him and pressed him hard. Yet his bow remained taut, and his arms were made agile by the hands of the Mighty One of Jacob, by the name of the Shepherd, the Rock of Israel, by the God of your father, who will help you, by the Almighty who will bless you with blessings of heaven above." (Genesis 49:22-25)

Good and Bad Shepherds

Rulers are naturally deemed the shepherds of their subjects, and in the prophetic writings, we see examples of both positive and negative embodiments for this.

Jeremiah speaks harshly of the rulers, when the nation of Judah is conquered and its people carried away in exile:

"For the shepherds are stupid, and do not inquire of the LORD;
Therefore they have not prospered, and all their flock is scattered." (Jeremiah 10:21)

"Woe to the shepherds who destroy and scatter the sheep of my pasture! Says the Lord. Therefore thus says the LORD, the God of Israel, concerning the shepherds who shepherd my people: It is you who have scattered my flock, and have driven them away, and you have not attended to them. So I will attend to you for your evil doings, says the LORD." (Jeremiah 23:1-2)

Jeremiah does offer the promise of restoration for God's flock:

"Then I myself will gather the remnant of my flock out of all the lands where I have driven them, and I will bring them back to their fold, and they shall be fruitful and multiply. I will raise up shepherds over them who will shepherd them, and they shall not fear any longer, or be dismayed, nor shall any be missing, says the LORD. (Jeremiah 23:3-4)

The 34th chapter of Ezekiel gives a close consideration to the same problem with the kings of Israel. God expected these rulers to care for the people as would a shepherd, but instead they have abused the people.

"Thus says the Lord GOD: Ah, you shepherds of Israel who have been feeding yourselves! Should not shepherds feed the sheep?" (Ezekiel 34:2-3)

The sad fate of God's flock is described: *"My sheep were scattered, they wandered over all the mountains and on every high hill; my sheep were scattered over all the face of the earth, with no one to search or seek for them." (Ezekiel 34:6)*

And, again, the LORD promises restoration: *"I myself will search for my sheep, and will seek them out. As shepherds seek out their flocks when they are among their scattered sheep, so I will seek out my sheep. I will rescue them from all the places to which they have been scattered on a day of clouds and thick darkness." (Ezekiel 34:11-12)*

The chapter continues with more assurances of God's future care for the sheep, including a shepherd in the line of King David, to lead them. God will offer peace for those in his care, concluding with this covenantal promise: *"You are my sheep, the sheep of my pasture and I am your God, says the Lord GOD." (Ezekiel 34:31)*

The prophet Isaiah also promises God's own care of his people as their shepherd. These may sound familiar to you as the lyrics of Handel's "Messiah".

"He will feed his flock like a shepherd; he will gather the lambs in his arms, and carry them in his bosom, and gently lead the mother sheep." (Isaiah 40:11)

Comforting Shepherd

Among the most memorized verses of the Bible, as well as the most recited during funeral services, we would include the Twenty-third Psalm. If I but begin the liturgy, how many of you could continue:

"The Lord is my shepherd . . ."

If your memory falters, find Psalm 23 in the middle of the Old Testament of your Bible and read on.

This is not the only psalm that features a good shepherd; it is a recurring theme.

"O save your people, and bless your heritage;
Be their shepherd, and carry them forever." (Psalm 28:9)

"Then he led out his people like sheep,
And guided them in the wilderness like a flock." (Psalm 78:52)

"For he is our God,
And we are the people of his pasture,
And the sheep of his hand." (Psalm 95:7)

"Know that the LORD is God.
It is he that made us, and we are his;
We are his people, and the sheep of his pasture." (Psalm 100:3)

Rejoice, for I have found my sheep that was lost.

Among the beloved parables that Luke relates in his gospel account, the 15th chapter, with its trilogy of lost things (a sheep, a coin, and a son), contains a conscientious shepherd who might be Jesus himself. When the shepherd discerns one of his one hundred sheep has wandered away, he seeks it. *"When he has found it, he lays it on his shoulders and rejoices. And when he comes home, he calls together his friends and neighbors, saying to them, 'Rejoice with me, for I have found my sheep that was lost.'" (Luke 15:5-7)*

John picks up the good shepherd/bad shepherd dichotomy that we found in Ezekiel.

"Very truly, I tell you, anyone who does not enter the sheepfold by the gate but climbs in by another way is a thief and a bandit. The one who enters by the gate is the shepherd of the sheep." (John 10:1-2)

So, the one the sheep will not follow, and whose voice they do not know, and from whom they run, is a stranger. The one who knows the sheep by name and leads them is the shepherd whom the sheep follow *"because they know his voice." (John 10:4)*

John further relates that a hired hand, who is not the owner, will leave the sheep in danger and run away. The good shepherd, however, is willing to give his own life to keep his sheep safe. With Jesus speaking these words, we hear the layers of meaning:

"And I lay down my life for the sheep. I have other sheep that do not belong to this fold. I must bring them also, and they will listen to my voice. So there will be one flock, one shepherd." (John 10:15-17)

The bottom line is that Jesus is *"the good shepherd"*. *(John 10:14)*

The Shepherd Lamb

In the NRSV translation, there is only one English occurrence of shepherd in Revelation. Ironically, the shepherd is identified as the Lamb!

Many of us have a common understanding that Jesus is the Lamb of God, but that is likely from our Sunday liturgies, rather than reading the gospels! Only in John, in his first chapter, do we hear, from John the Baptist, that Jesus is the "Lamb of God". The main New Testament book that shows Jesus as the Lamb of God is Revelation, where there are multiple references to this.

Ironically, the Lamb of God is also our shepherd: *"For the Lamb at the center of the throne will be their shepherd, and he will guide them to springs of the water of life." (Revelation 7:17)*

If we were reading Revelation in its original Greek, however, we would find two other instances of the word shepherd. The English translators, have chosen, instead, to render these both as "rule"!

"And she gave birth to a son, a male child, who is to rule [shepherd] all the nations." (Revelation 12:5)

"From his mouth comes a sharp sword with which to strike down the nations, and he will rule [shepherd] them with a rod of iron." (Revelation 19:15)

Pondering

With more of us living in urban areas rather than rural, does the metaphor of a shepherd still hold up well?

Are there any current elected officials whom you would consider to be shepherding citizens well?

I am the resurrection and the life.

John 11:25

What does scripture tell us about
the resurrection and the life?

Although they are integrally related, there are two parts to this metaphor, and we will examine each for their references in the Bible. For the concept of "life", we will expand that to "breath of life".

In the Torah

The Ruah

Yet again we find the creation story in Genesis laying down key theological concepts that will echo throughout scripture.

"In the beginning when God created the heavens and the earth, the earth was a formless void and darkness covered the face of the deep, while a wind from God swept over the face of the waters." (Genesis 1:1-2)

What do we learn about God from these verses? A lesson in Hebrew vocabulary will help with that question. The "wind" described is the concept *"ruah"*. It can be a wind or a breath or a spirit. The word even epitomizes its meaning, if you hold your hand right over your mouth and say the word *"ruah"*. Did you feel the air moving?

When the Old Testament translators encounter *"ruah"*, they might select any of the three English words, but it is rarely capitalized (not "Spirit"). Nevertheless, for Christian readers, the Holy Spirit is clearly present here.

Still in the first chapter of Genesis, we have the tale of God creating day and night, earth and seas, vegetation and animals, and ultimately humankind. When God blesses humankind, God also instructs them, *"And to every beast of the earth, and to every bird of the air, and to everything that creeps on the earth, everything that has the breath of life, I have given every green plant for food." (Genesis 1:30)*

The presence of this *"ruah"*, this breath, then, is both the source and the animating force for creation. This holds true for the second creation story that begins in the second chapter of Genesis. (See for yourself; there are two separate stories, with different chronologies!)

"Then the LORD God formed man from the dust of the ground, and breathed into his nostrils the breath of life; and the man became a living being." (Genesis 2:7)

As more people populate God's creation, God learns about them as they are learning about God. The lesson of Noah's generation was a hard lesson. Soon thereafter, God makes a pronouncement: *"Then the LORD said, 'My spirit shall not abide in mortals forever, for they are flesh; their days shall be one hundred twenty years.'" (Genesis 6:3)* The "spirit", of course, is the *"ruah"*, the very breath of life.

There is a breadth to this breath, as we discover in *Exodus 31*, in which the LORD tells Moses of the talents that have been given to assorted artisans: *"See, I have called by name Bezalel son of Uri son of Hur, of the tribe of Judah: and I have filled him with the divine spirit, with ability, intelligence, and knowledge in every kind of craft." (Exodus 31:2-3)*

Throughout the Hebrew Bible, when God calls particular individuals to carry out his will, it is often reported that these people are infused with *"ruah."* For example, this happened to Othniel, Caleb's younger brother: *"The spirit of the LORD came upon him, and he judged Israel." (Judges 3:10)*

31

Breath of God

The prophets also refer to God's "ruah" with frequency.

"The spirit of the LORD shall rest on him,
The spirit of wisdom and understanding,
The spirit of counsel and might,
The spirit of knowledge and the fear of the LORD." (Isaiah 11:2)
"Thus says God, the LORD,
who created the heavens and stretched them out,
who spread out the earth and what comes from it,
who gives breath to the people upon it
and spirit to those who walk in it." (Isaiah 42:5)

The *"ruah"* has a starring role in prophet Ezekiel's vision of the valley filled with dry bones. God tells Ezekiel to prophesy to the bones that the LORD would "put breath" in them and they would "live". Ezekiel complies, and then it happens, with a rushing of winds. God speaks, *"Come from the four winds, O breath, and breathe upon these slain, that they may live." (Ezekiel 37:9)*

The LORD then tells Ezekiel that the vision represented the people of Israel, whose hope had been lost, just as the bones were dried up. So, God then promises: *"I am going to open your graves, and bring you up from your graves, O my people; and I will bring you back to the land of Israel. And you shall know that I am the LORD, when I open your graves, and bring you up from your graves, O my people. I will put my spirit within you, and you shall live, and I will place you on your own soil; then you shall know that I, the LORD, have spoken and will act, says the LORD." (Ezekiel 37:12-14)*

Other prophets offer similar words of promise and hope:

"Your dead shall live, their corpses shall rise.
O dwellers in the dust, awake and sing for joy!
For your dew is a radiant dew,
And the earth will give birth to those long dead." (Isaiah 26:19)

In the Kethuvim

The Vapor

The belief in the Old Testament is that when one died, *"and the dust returns to the earth as it was, and the breath returns to God who gave it. Vanity of vanities, says the Teacher; all is vanity." (Ecclesiastes 12:7-8)*

A fascinating thing about this last well-known verse is that "vanity" is from the Hebrew word *"hebel"*, which better translates as "vapor" or "breath"!

In the Gospels

The Pneuma

The word that has permeated the Old Testament as spirit, the *"ruah"*, translates into Greek, the language of the New Testament, as *"pneuma"* (πνευμα). Our English word pneumatic, meaning air-driven, comes from this. In the New Testament, we usually read the translation as Spirit or Holy Spirit, and notice it is now capitalized.

The Spirit, *"pneuma"*, is very active in the New Testament! Luke especially, in his two-volume set, *"The Gospel According to Luke"* and *"The Acts of the Apostles"*, puts forth the Holy Spirit as a definite character in the story. John the Baptist is filled with the Holy Spirit (*Luke 1:15*); Mary is overshadowed by the Holy Spirit (*Luke 1:35*), Mary's kinswoman Elizabeth is filled with it (*Luke 1:41*), her husband Zechariah is filled with it (*Luke 1:67*), and that's just chapter one!

Resurrection

Two Greek words describe the concept of resurrection in the New Testament. First, we have *anastasis* (αναστασις), a noun, which is "standing up" or resurrection. Second, we have *egeiro* (εγειρω), a verb, that is "raise" or "awake".

A righteous man, Simeon, on whom the Holy Spirit also rested, blessed infant Jesus and his parents, then said, *"This child is destined for the falling and the rising of many in Israel." (Luke 2:34)* The word shown as "rising" is the Greek *anastasis*, so we definitely have two layers of meaning here.

Jesus tends to speak with double entendre throughout John. An early example is in the second chapter: *"The Jews then said to him, 'What sign can you show us for doing this?' Jesus answered them, 'Destroy this temple, and in three days I will raise it up.' The Jews then said, 'This temple has been under construction for forty-six years, and will you raise it up in three days?' But he was speaking of the temple of his body. After he was raised from the dead, his disciples remembered that he had said this; and they believed the scripture and the word that Jesus had spoken." (John 2:18-22)*

Now, here's a curious paragraph in Matthew, that no other evangelist reported. Wouldn't it be nice to hear a sermon about this:

"Then Jesus cried again with a loud voice and breathed his last. At that moment the curtain of the temple was torn in two, from top to bottom. The earth shook, and the rocks were split. The tombs were also opened, and many bodies of the saints who had fallen asleep were raised. After his resurrection they came out of the tombs and entered the holy city and appeared to many." (Matthew 27:50-53)

Back to evangelist John, we have many lengthy teaching monologues by Jesus, sometimes to the crowd and sometimes to just his disciples. Just after Jesus makes his "bread of life" statement in the sixth chapter of John, we also learn more about resurrection:

"Everything that the Father gives me will come to me, and anyone who comes to me I will never drive away; for I have come down from heaven, not to do my own will, but the will of him who sent me, that I should lose nothing of all that he has given me, but raise it up on the last day. This is indeed the will of my Father, that all who see the Son and believe in him may have eternal life; and I will raise them up on the last day." (John 6:37-40)

But, where do we find the fifth metaphor of our series? In the eleventh chapter of John, we hear the story of Jesus' bringing his friend Lazarus back from the dead. Only John records this story. It is during this episode, when Jesus speaks to Lazarus' sister Martha, just prior to calling Lazarus forth from his tomb, that we have this particular conversation:

"Martha said to Jesus, 'Lord, if you had been here, my brother would not have died. But even now I know that God will give you whatever you ask of him.' Jesus said to her, 'Your brother will rise again.' Martha said to him, 'I know that he will rise again in the resurrection on the last day.' Jesus said to her, 'I am the resurrection and the life. Those who believe in me, even though they die, will live, and everyone who lives and believes in me will never die.'" (John 11:21-26)

Pondering

Do you agree that there is an integral relationship between "resurrection" and "breath of life"?

Is there a distinction, and how would you explain it, between Lazarus being brought forth from the dead and Jesus' own resurrection from the dead, which is considered the first resurrection?

I am the way, the truth, and the life.

John 14:6

What does scripture tell us about the way, the truth, and the life?

The English word "way" appears in the New Revised Standard Version of the Bible over 700 times. Sometimes, however, a word is no more than its literal meaning; in this case, the common noun "way" usually stands for a pathway or a direction. There are also occasions when it is part of a phrase you would expect in the Bible, such as "the way of the Lord".

In the Torah

The Lord's Way

Even before the commandments were given, it was important to *"keep the way of the LORD". (Genesis 18:19)* In this story, Abraham, who is very advanced in years, has been given the promise of a son. Then there is a curious interior monologue in which it appears God is talking to himself: *"The LORD said, 'Shall I hide from Abraham what I am about to do, seeing that Abraham shall become a great and mighty nation, and all the nations of the earth shall be blessed in him?'" (Genesis 18:17-18)*

God answers his own question and states that Abraham has been chosen to *"keep the way of the LORD by doing righteousness and justice." (Genesis 18:19)*

After receiving God's commandments, as part of the covenant with God, the people were expected to *"take care to walk in the way of the LORD." (Judges 2:22)* It becomes clear in the book of Judges that this is a difficult thing for them to manage, and the people continually fall into cycles of doing *"what was evil in the sight of the LORD." (Judges 2:11; 3:7; 4:1; 6:1; 10:6; 13:1)*

"They soon turned aside from the way in which their ancestors had walked, who had obeyed the commandments of the LORD; they did not follow their example."

(Judges 2:17) Each time, the people would cry out to God, and God would send a deliverer to them.

<u>In the Nevi'im</u>

Way of the Lord

As the prophet Isaiah delivers oracles to encourage the people to prepare for a return from exile, *"the way of the LORD"* is a common phrase. In the following passage, this includes smoothing out an actual highway, right? Or, do you also see this as a metaphor:

"A voice cries out:
'In the wilderness, prepare the way of the LORD,
make straight in the desert a highway for our God.
Every valley shall be lifted up,
And every mountain and hill be made low;
The uneven ground shall become level,
And the rough places a plain.
Then the glory of the LORD shall be revealed,
And all the people shall see it together,
For the mouth of the LORD has spoken.'" (Isaiah 40:3-5)

A restoration is definitely the plan:

"Thus says the LORD, your Redeemer, the Holy One of Israel:
I am the LORD your God,
Who teaches you for your own good,
Who leads you in the way you should go." (Isaiah 48:17)

Prophet Ezekiel speaks to the people about accountability:

"But if the wicked turn away from all their sins that they have committed and keep all my statutes and do what is lawful and right, they shall surely live; they shall not die. None of the transgressions that they have committed shall be remembered

against them; for the righteousness that they have done they shall live." (Ezekiel 18:21-22)

The people, like spoiled children, reply, "*The way of the Lord is unfair.*" (Ezekiel 18:25) God, the parent, responds, "*Is my way unfair? Is it not your ways that are unfair? When the righteous turn away from their righteousness and commit iniquity, they shall die for it; for the iniquity that they have committed they shall die. Again, when the wicked turn away from the wickedness they have committed and do what is lawful and right, they shall save their life.*" (Ezekiel 18:25-27)

In the Kethuvim

The Moral Way

Proverbs is a compilation of helpful insights for how to cope with life in a moral way. The word "way" represented a standard concept for a lifestyle choice in the Hebrew tradition. Values such as honesty, hard work, diligence, trust in God, and righteous behavior should bring prosperity.

We hear echoes of the words of the prophets:

"*The way of the LORD is a stronghold for the upright,*
but destruction for evildoers." (Proverbs 10:29)

Teaching the Way

Jesus is sometimes called "Rabbi", which is Teacher, in the gospels. As such, people ask him questions about moral issues. Sometimes it is Pharisees or Sadducees, differing religious sects of Jews, who ask questions in attempts to trick Jesus.

"Then they sent to him some Pharisees and some Herodians to trap him in what he said. And they came and said to him, 'Teacher, we know that you are sincere, and show deference to no one; for you do not regard people with partiality, but teach the way of God in accordance with truth. Is it lawful to pay taxes to the emperor, or not?'" (Mark 12:14) Jesus is not outwitted by any questions. In this case, upon asking to see a coin, and asking whose likeness is imprinted upon it, he responds, *"Give to the emperor the things that are the emperor's, and to God the things that are God's."* (Mark 12:17)

In John's Gospel, before his account of Jesus' arrest, four chapters are devoted to what is known as the "Farewell Discourse" of Jesus, in which he consoles and prays for the disciples. Jesus tells them he will bring them to himself, so that they may be with him always.

"Thomas said to him, 'Lord, we do not know where you are going. How can we know the way?' Jesus said to him, 'I am the way, and the truth, and the life. No one comes to the Father except through me.'" (John 14:5-6)

The most helpful thing to remember about Jesus as the way, is that Jesus is a two-way street! Not only is Jesus a way to God, but Jesus is the way God comes to us.

Following the Way

As followers of Jesus grew in number, they had no specific name; the title Christians would not be used during Jesus' lifetime or even very soon after it. According to the book of Acts, they were just known as followers of the Way.

"Meanwhile Saul, still breathing threats and murder against the disciples of the Lord, went to the high priest and asked him for letters to the synagogues at Damascus, so that if he found any who belonged to the Way, men or women, he might bring them bound to Jerusalem." (Acts 9:1-2)

Very soon, we learn that Saul has a conversion experience and he himself becomes a follower of the Way, with a name change, as well: Paul. By the conclusion of Acts, Paul is a great defender and missionary of the Way.

"But this I admit to you, that according to the Way, which they call a sect, I worship the God of our ancestors, believing everything laid down according to the law or written in the prophets. I have a hope in God—a hope that they themselves also accept—that there will be a resurrection of both the righteous and the unrighteousness. Therefore I do my best always to have a clear conscience toward God and all people." (Acts 24:14-16)

We have examined various references to the word "way" in scripture, but the metaphor does not end there. We also must consider "the truth". As you can imagine, the word is found throughout the Old and New Testaments. Here is an example that combines both our words:

"Make me to know your ways, O LORD;
teach me your paths.
Lead me in your truth, and teach me,
For you are the God of my salvation;
For you I wait all day long." (Psalm 25:4-5)

The Faithful and True

Truth, of course, is the opposite of falsehood. Interestingly, the adjective "true" has a richer possibility than just being the antonym of "false". It can also mean "straight" or "correct", as in the true course of a ship.

John of Patmos opens his Revelation with a description of the Son of Man. We learn this is the exalted Christ, and one of his attributes is that *"from his mouth came a sharp, two-edged sword." (Revelation 1:16)* We know, don't we, what comes from the mouth of Jesus; it is the Word of God; it is Truth.

The attributes of the Christ we read about in the first chapter, are then picked up in the letters to the seven churches, found in the next two chapters. It is in the letter to the church in Laodicea that we hear echoes of the description above: *"And to the angel of the church in Laodicea write: The words of the Amen, the faithful and true witness, the origin of God's creation." (Revelation 3:14)* And, how did God's creation come into being? It was spoken into existence.

Each of the seven churches receiving letters also receives promises that are kept in the final chapters of Revelation. After several vision cycles of seven elements each, the scene changes to the throne of heaven: *"Then I saw heaven opened, and there was a white horse! Its rider is called Faithful and True." (Revelation 19:11)* This rider has a sword coming out of his mouth, so we know it is Jesus, and he is identified by name: *"and his name is called The Word of God." (Revelation 19:13)*

<u>Pondering</u>

Have you heard this metaphor, *"I am the way . . ."* used by people to suggest that only by "coming to Jesus" will one be "saved"? I do believe that looking at the phrase through the lens of the grammar of the original Greek text, one might find this passage not as much of a proof text to show "who's in and who's out"!

In Greek, every noun is always preceded by a definite article…"the". There are no indefinite articles in Greek (such as "a", or "an"). Therefore, in translating, there is often the possibility that a noun is describing something in general or something in particular. For example, Greek would always be, "the evil". This could be translated as evil, in general, or the evil one, in particular, with "one" being an understood qualifier.

When Jesus says, "I am the way," it does not mean, in Greek, that he is the only way! It does mean, in Greek, that he is "a" way, either in general or in particular! Without a qualifier indicating that this was the one and only way, we could be mistaken in assuming that this statement functions to exclude anyone who might approach God in a different way!

Greek also has a peculiar way of indicating qualifiers to a noun. In fact, it is entirely possible in the sentence, *"I am the way, the truth, and the life,"* that "life" is the object noun, while both "way" and "truth" function as qualifying words. That means, an acceptable translation could be, "I am the true way to life."

What do you think about these possibilities?

I am the vine.

John 15:5

What does scripture tell us about the vine and branches?

The vine and the branches metaphor from John 15:5, "*I am the vine, you are the branches,*" reaches back to a rich Jewish tradition of the people of Israel being God's vineyard. The Hebrew Bible is filled with images of this. Grapes, figs, and olives grow well in a Mediterranean environment, so it is an image to which the people could relate.

The Torah

The First Vineyard

Right after the flood that Noah and the ark of animals endured for forty days and forty nights, God made a covenant with Noah, his descendants, and every living creature that survived in the ark. God signed this promise with a rainbow. (*Genesis 9:8-17*)

It was immediately thereafter that Noah was the first to plant a vineyard. (*Genesis 9:20*) The predominant patriarchs of Genesis (Abraham, Isaac, Esau, Jacob and his sons) were herders, as were the Israelites who wandered for forty years in the wilderness after escaping from bondage in Egypt, so we do not find much more about vineyards in the Torah, although there are provisions about them in the law code of Leviticus.

The Nevi'im

The Vineyard of the Beloved

The prophetic writings begin long after the people had settled in Canaan, the land of "*milk and honey*" (*Exodus 33:3*), the land of promise, and the references to God's people being his vineyard increase. A particularly long passage establishing the people of Israel and Judah as God's vineyard is the following canticle from Isaiah. A canticle is a song found in the Bible.

"Let me sing for my beloved my love-song concerning his vineyard:
My beloved had a vineyard on a very fertile hill.
He dug it and cleared it of stones, and planted it with choice vines;
He built a watchtower in the middle of it,
And hewed out a wine vat in it; he expected it to yield grapes,
but it yielded wild grapes." (Isaiah 5:1-2)

In Jerusalem, God's Temple had been built by Solomon upon a steep hill known as Mt. Zion since the time of his father King David. The name Zion is synonymous with the dwelling of God. In the verses above, the hill is the Temple Mount, or Zion, and the watchtower is very likely the Temple. God expected his people to live in harmony with the Torah, but the people proved to be wilder in behavior.

"And now, inhabitants of Jerusalem and people of Judah,
judge between me and my vineyard.
What more was there to do for my vineyard that I have not done in it?
When I expected it to yield grapes, why did it yield wild grapes?" (Isaiah 5:3-4)

The prevailing thinking of the people during the time of the prophets was theocentric. That is, whatever happened to you or your tribe or your country, whether good or bad, was at the direct hand of God. When unpleasant things happened, these were mostly seen as punishments sent by God. There are Old Testament books that refute this notion, two examples being Job and Ecclesiastes. The prophets Isaiah and Jeremiah, however, definitely proclaim a link between the wild behavior of the "grapes" and what will befall them at the hands of the Assyrians and Babylonians.

"And now I will tell you what I will do to my vineyard.
I will remove its hedge, and it shall be devoured;
I will break down its wall, and it shall be trampled down." (Isaiah 5:5)

In no uncertain terms, Isaiah identifies the people of Israel and Judah as the LORD's vineyard, in whom there were high expectations:

"For the vineyard of the LORD of hosts is the house of Israel,
and the people of Judah are his pleasant planting;

he expected justice, but saw bloodshed;
righteousness, but heard a cry!" (Isaiah 5:7)

And in equally clear terms, Isaiah proclaims the punishment:

"Therefore my people will go into exile." (Isaiah 5:13)

The prophet Jeremiah echoes similar sentiments:

"Yet I planted you as a choice vine, from the purest stock.
How then did you turn degenerate and become a wild vine?" (Jeremiah 2:21)

Not only has the vine become "wild", but the trees are not bearing fruit.

"When I wanted to gather them, says the LORD, there are no grapes on the vine,
nor figs on the fig tree; even the leaves are withered, and what I gave them has passed
away from them." (Jeremiah 8:13)

The prophets' messages could sound like thunderbolts of doom for the people, but the prophets also offered the LORD's promising words of comfort and restoration.

"Return, O Israel, to the LORD your God,
for you have stumbled because of your iniquity." (Hosea 14:1)

"I will heal their disloyalty; I will love them freely,
For my anger has turned from them.
I will be like the dew to Israel; he shall blossom like the lily,
he shall strike root like the forests of Lebanon.
His shoots shall spread out;
his beauty shall be like the olive tree,
and his fragrance like that of Lebanon.
They shall again live beneath my shadow,
they shall flourish as a garden,
they shall blossom like the vine,
their fragrance shall be like the wine of Lebanon." (Hosea 14:4-7)

The Beloved as a Vineyard

One of the more controversial scrolls in the collection called The Writings is *The Song of Solomon*, also known as *The Song of Songs*.

The only reason for attributing it to Solomon was because of his purported great number of wives. It is actually an erotic love poem that almost did not make it into the canon of the Bible. Only because it was read as a metaphor of God's love for Israel did it make the cut.

Botanic terms of endearment are used throughout the poem—rose of Sharon, lily of the valley, an apple tree, pomegranates, saffron, cinnamon, frankincense and other spices, and, yes, *"clusters of the vine"* (*Song of Solomon 7:8*) and *"the best wine."* (*Song of Solomon 7:9*)

It is probably the allusion to a vineyard, which had been the metaphor for God's people, that tipped the vote for inclusion of this book in the Bible.

"My vineyard, my very own, is for myself." (Song of Solomon 8:12)

The Vinegrower and the Vine

All three synoptic gospels have the Parable of the Vineyard (*Matthew 21:33-46; Mark 12:1-9; Luke 20:9-19*), in which the story is set in a vineyard, but the moral is actually about landlords and tenants, and the teaching is more allegorical to God, the prophets, and Jesus.

The synoptics also offer the enacted parable of a fig tree (*Matthew 21:18-21; Mark 11:19-21; Luke 13:6-7*), in which Jesus withers a tree that had no fruit. This is also seen as an allegory, one directed toward the Temple officials perhaps.

Now for the "*I am the vine*" metaphor from John. The 15th chapter of that gospel opens with Jesus telling his disciples, "*I am the true vine and my Father is the vinegrower. He removes every branch in me that bears no fruit. Every branch that bears fruit he prunes to make it bear more fruit.*" (*John 15:1-2*) This definitely harkens back to the Isaiah passages of God and his vineyard.

Interestingly, Jesus identifies his disciples as branches on the vine that is himself, within God's vineyard. Indeed, Jesus says, "*My Father is glorified by this, that you bear much fruit and become my disciples.*" (*John 15:8*)

Jesus' "I am . . ." metaphor is part of this discourse: "*I am the vine, you are the branches. Those who abide in me and I in them bear much fruit, because apart from me you can do nothing.*" (*John 15:5*)

This ends the seventh and final "I Am the . . ." metaphor from John about Jesus' identity. But, with a little botanic poetic license, this gardening image can be examined through another window to the Word.

God the Gardener

Let us set aside figs and grapes for the moment and take an excursion into the whole of scripture to find another botanical metaphor, one that both opens and closes our Bible. I am speaking of the tree of life.

Two Trees

In the beginning, when God had formed man *"from the dust of the ground, and breathed into his nostrils the breath of life . . .God also planted a garden in Eden." (Genesis 2:7-8)*

In addition to all the pleasant fruit trees in the garden, God planted *"the tree of life also in the midst of the garden, and the tree of the knowledge of good and evil." (Genesis 2:9)* God commands his human, *"You may freely eat of every tree of the garden; but of the tree of knowledge of good and evil you shall not eat, for in the day that you eat of it you shall die." (Genesis 2:16-17)*

The rest of the story is pretty familiar, right? The crafty serpent entices the woman to taste the fruit of the tree of the knowledge of good and evil, she succumbs, then she encourages the man to do the same. The next thing we know, God is strolling among his trees, looking for the pair, but they have hidden themselves from fear of what they had done.

Here's a note of interest, the scripture never tells us this was an apple tree. It was a translation pun made by Jerome, when he wrote the Latin translation known as the Vulgate in the 4th century. In Latin, *malum* can be both "bad" and "apple". Art of the medieval and Renaissance eras will sometimes depict different fruit being taken by Eve; some paintings show figs (after all, they covered themselves with fig leaves!), and another possibility depicted is the pomegranate.

In any event, for their disobedience, Adam and Eve are expelled from the garden. Then God proclaims, *"See, the man has become like one of us, knowing good and evil; and now, he might reach out his hand and take also from the tree of life, and eat, and live forever"*—*"therefore the LORD God sent him forth from the garden of Eden, to till the ground from which he was taken. He drove out the man; and at the east of the garden of Eden he placed the cherubim, and a sword flaming and turning to guard the way to the tree of life." (Genesis 3:22-24)*

A Tree Foreshadowed

Another mention of tree must be made, as its ominous usage portends future events.

"When someone is convicted of a crime punishable by death and is executed, and you hang him on a tree, his corpse must not remain all night upon the tree; you shall bury him that same day, for anyone hung on a tree is under God's curse." (Deuteronomy 21:22-23)

God Plants Another Tree

The prophet Ezekiel offers several allegories before his concluding chapters of his Temple Vision. One of the most beautiful allegories is about a tree, in which life will flourish, and this is interpreted in a messianic way by Christians:

"Thus says the Lord GOD:
I myself will take a sprig from the top of a cedar; I will set it out.
I will break off a tender one from the topmost of its young twigs;
I myself will plant it on a high and lofty mountain.
On the mountain height of Israel I will plant it,
in order that it may produce boughs and bear fruit,
and become a noble cedar.
Under it every kind of bird will live;
in the shade of its branches will nest winged creatures of every kind.
All the trees of the field shall know that I am the LORD.
I bring low the high tree, I make high the low tree;
I dry up the green tree and make the dry tree flourish.
I the LORD have spoken; I will accomplish it." (Ezekiel 17:22-24)

As Ezekiel relates his vision of the new temple, he describes ever increasing water flowing from below the threshold of this temple that became a river that could not be crossed (*Ezekiel 47:1-5*) Then he is shown amazing trees:

"On the banks, on both sides of the river, there will grow all kinds of trees for food. Their leaves will not wither nor their fruit fail, but they will bear fresh fruit every month, because the water for them flows from the sanctuary. Their fruit will be for food, and their leaves for healing." (Ezekiel 47:12) This obviously foreshadows another tree to be found in the New Jerusalem described in Revelation.

53

Torah as Tree

The tree of life is an idiom found regularly in Proverbs. Speaking of wisdom, we learn: *"She is a tree of life to those who lay hold of her; those who hold her fast are called happy." (Proverbs 3:18)* For the Jews, the Torah itself was considered a tree of life!

The botanic metaphor continues to be applied to righteous behavior, because it suggests longevity:

"The fruit of the righteous is a tree of life, but violence takes lives away." (Proverbs 11:30)

"A gentle tongue is a tree of life, but perverseness in it breaks the spirit." (Proverbs 15:4)

In Psalms, the liturgies sing of the animation of all creation in thanksgiving to God: *"Then shall all the trees of the forest sing for joy before the LORD; for he is coming." (Psalm 96:12)*

Twelve-Fruited Tree of Life

The conclusion to our Bible may be found in the final chapters of Revelation, with the glorious vision witnessed by John of Patmos.

"Then the angel showed me the river of the water of life, bright as crystal, flowing from the throne of God and of the Lamb though the middle of the street of the city. On either side of the river is the tree of life with its twelve kinds of fruit, producing its fruit each month; and the leaves of the tree are for the healing of the nations." (Revelation 22:1-2)

Whereas access to the tree of life in God's garden in Eden had been prevented by the flaming sword of the cherubim, now as the vision of John of Patmos closes, we glimpse what the coming of the Lord will offer:

"Blessed are those who wash their robes, so that they will have the right to the tree of life and may enter the city by the gates." (Revelation 22:14)

The tree that made its appearance early in Genesis is back in the holy city of God that has come down from heaven, the New Jerusalem, where God will dwell with his people.

What is most fascinating, however, is that there are two words used in the New Testament Greek for "tree". One is *dendron* (δενδρον), as used in the gospels and even in Revelation 9:4. There is another word in Greek, *xylon* (ξυλον), that is the word John of Patmos used in Revelation 22:2. Why the different word choice? In English, we might translate the two words as "timber" vs "lumber"—one is standing and one is cut.

John of Patmos clearly knew the difference when he penned Revelation. The most uses of *xylon* are found in Acts, where it is used to describe the death of Jesus by "hanging him on a tree". There is no question that this tree is the cross of crucifixion.

"The God of our ancestors raised up Jesus, whom you had killed by hanging him on a tree." (Acts 5:30)

"We are witnesses to all that he did both in Judea and in Jerusalem. They put him to death by hanging him on a tree; but God raised him on the third day." (Acts 10:39)

Our final vision of the tree of life, and our last encounter with a tree in the Bible, is not the tree from the Garden of Eden! It is instead the tree that has brought healing and redemption to God's creation. It is a reimagining of creation with the center of the story as the real tree of life, and that is the cross that leads to life. That is the crux of the story. Thanks be to God!

Were there any surprises for you in this chapter?

Which works better as a comparison of the two—the vine or the tree of life? Explain your reasons.

Catechism of the Lamb

The windows to the Word that we have considered are part of a larger scope and sequence presented by evangelist John. This chapter will consider what may have been the author's intention.

As noted toward the beginning of this text, John's Gospel has a unique eye. There is a lot left out, when compared to the synoptic gospels. There is no birth story, no baptism tale, no temptation account, no exorcisms, no parables, no Sermon the Mount, no Lord's Prayer, and no Transfiguration. These omissions seem odd, but that's not all to say.

There are also lots of additions to the content. It has been estimated that 90% of this gospel is not found elsewhere—beginning with the wedding at Cana and concluding with a post-resurrection breakfast on a beach. Only this gospel calls Jesus the Lamb of God. (*John 1:36*)

We have already commented upon the seven distinctive metaphors found in John. Another characteristic is that John does not offer any miracle stories. Instead he refers to "signs" which Jesus performed, seven of them specifically, to show the glory of God. When we hear "glory", we might think it is an attribute, like the fame and glory a modern-day athlete or movie star might possess, but that is not the Biblical meaning. The Hebrew word *Shekinah* is translated throughout the Old Testament as *"the glory of God"*; its more precise translation in the Hebrew Bible is *"the Presence of God"*. Each of Jesus' seven signs of the glory of God gives us a glimpse into what life in the very presence of God might look like.

The first sign (*John 2:1-11*) is the wedding at Cana—with themes of joy and abundance, this recalls the prophecy of Amos, which tells of a time to come in which *"the mountains shall drip with sweet wine, and all the hills shall flow with it."* (*Amos 9:13-14*)

59

The second sign (*John 4:46-54*) is the healing of an official's son.

The third sign (*John 5:1-9*) is another healing, this time of a lame man. This recalls an Isaiah passage that states, "*Then the lame shall leap like a deer.*" (*Isaiah 35:6*)

The fourth sign (*John 6:1-14*) is the feeding of the five thousand. This is the only sign that is found in all four of the gospels, which speaks to its centrality. It involves bread that is broken, blessed, and given, perhaps reminding us of holy communion or eucharist.

The fifth sign (*John 6:16-21*) is Jesus' calming of a stormy sea. According to the Old Testament, all of nature's elements are under God's command. Psalm 107 sings of the LORD who controls the storm-tossed sea.

The sixth sign (*John 9*) tells of a man born blind, but as promised in Isaiah, "*Then the eyes of the blind shall be opened.*" (*Isaiah 35:5*) The man's vision is restored.

The seventh sign (*John 11*) is the raising of Lazarus from the dead. All seven signs are symbolic actions revealing God's glory and the abundant life that attends the presence of God.

From the first chapter in John, when Jesus asks what people are looking for, everyone is trying to figure out who he is. Essentially, the rest of the gospel is an answer to that, by giving us conversations and stories to show how people come to their own varied conclusions about who Jesus is. Some call him Rabbi, others Messiah, some the son of Joseph, or the King of Israel. Only one person gets the complete answer.

In a post-resurrection appearance of Jesus, we learn that disciple Thomas had not believed that the other disciples had seen Jesus one week earlier. When Thomas does see Jesus, Jesus invites Thomas to put his finger into Jesus' wound. (Actually, the Greek uses the verb "thrust" for Jesus' offer to Thomas!) Despite being called "Doubting

Thomas" for two millennia, in fact, Thomas is the very first person in John's entire gospel to make the true identification of Jesus. At this point, Thomas proclaims, *"My Lord and my God!"* (*John 20:28*) Thomas realizes that when he looks upon Jesus, he is seeing the face of God.

With this running theme of "Who do you say that I am?", John also offers us exactly seven instances of Jesus proclaiming solely, "I Am" (εγω ειμι). The Greek is not read with a predicate nominative; it would not translate as "I am he." When the Jews (or Judean authorities) heard Jesus saying "I Am," they heard outright blasphemy; they heard him claiming, "I Am God." Here are those instances:

The first time, in conversation with the Samaritan woman at a well, and she admits her believe in the coming of Christ, Jesus says, *"I Am."* (*John 4:26*)

The second time, when the disciples are caught in a storm on the sea and are terrified to see Jesus walking upon the water, Jesus tells them, *"I Am."* (*John 6:20*) When the New Revised Standard Version prints, *"It is I,"* then it has missed the theological point.

The third time, during the Festival of Booths, when the great golden Temple lamps are lighted, Jesus tells the crowd that he is the light of the world. The crowd asks him some questions, and he replies, *"I Am."* (*John 8:24*)

The fourth time, still in the Festival of Booths speech, people ask who he is and claim confusion so Jesus reiterates, once he's been lifted up, then they will realize, *"I Am."* (*John 8:28*)

The fifth time, Jesus tells the people that *"before Abraham was, I Am,"* and they then try to stone him, but he escapes. (*John 8:58*)

The sixth time, after washing the feet of his disciples, another story unique to John, Jesus states in his discourse to the disciples, *"I Am."* (*John 18*)

The seventh time, when Jesus is in the garden, and Judas approaches with the soldiers, Jesus says, "*I Am.*" He actually says this a symbolic three times in this situation. (*John 18:5,6,8*)

Scholars have noted there are specific parallels between what Jesus did and what Moses did in the Exodus narrative. The deliverance from the bondage of slavery was a defining time for the Israelites. The gospel of John provides seven examples of Jesus surpassing the deeds of Moses.

In *Exodus 7:17-21*, the water of the Nile is turned into blood as a warning; in *John 2:1-11*, Jesus turns water in wine as a blessing.

In *Exodus 14:21-31*, the waters of the sea are parted to allow the people to cross to safety; in *John 6:16-21*, Jesus controls the stormy sea, saving his disciples.

In *Exodus 17:1-7*, Moses struck a rock with his staff, and water gushed forth; in *John 19:34*, Jesus (who had claimed to offer living water) is pierced by a spear, and water gushes forth, along with his blood.

In *Exodus 16:2-26*, manna from heaven feeds the people in the wilderness; in *John 6:2-14*, Jesus, the bread of life, feeds five thousand from a few barley loaves.

In *Numbers 21:5-9*, Moses lifted up a bronze serpent upon a pole, so when people gazed upon it, they would not die of the bites of vipers; in *John 3:14-15*, Jesus says, "*And just as Moses lifted up the serpent in the wilderness, so must the Son of Man be lifted up, that whoever believes in him may have eternal life.*"

In the 20th chapter of Exodus, Moses is given the commandments; in *John 13:34*, Jesus gives a new commandment that we love one another as he has loved us.

Throughout the Torah, Moses was the people's guide to the promised land. In John, Jesus promises, *"And if I go and prepare a place for you, I will come again and will take you to myself, so that where I am, there you may be also."* (*John 14:3*) A promised land, indeed!

You might not be surprised to learn that there are also seven parallels to the creation story of Genesis. Evangelist John wants his audience to realize Jesus has sovereignty over creation.

John's gospel also brings forth the full annual cycle of Jewish festivals, from one Passover to the next. Jesus' ministry in John begins with the cleansing of the Temple, as told in chapter two. The synoptics place that event at the end of Jesus' ministry.

The next festival, the Festival of Weeks, marked the barley season, and we've already noted that Jesus feeds a multitude from barley loaves and calls himself the Bread of Life.

The Festival of Booths occurs in chapter seven. This holy festival included many prayers, including praying for rain during winter, for an end to sickness and death, for the Messiah to come, and for paradise to be restored. Daily, during the seven days of this festival, the priests performed an elaborate water ritual.

In Jerusalem, the Pool of Siloam (the one mentioned in *John 9:7*) is fed by water from the spring of Gihon. Coincidentally, one of the rivers named in paradise was Gihon (*Genesis 2:13*). A priest fills a golden pitcher with water from the Pool; this is then poured over the altar, with the hope that the River Gihon from paradise might gush forth right there in the Temple (where the Jews believe creation had occurred) in a glorious restoration of paradise. This is repeated for seven days. [To learn more about these traditions, do an internet search for *Simchat Beit Hashoeivah* and/or *Nisuch ha-Mayim*.]

During the middle of this particular festival, Jesus went to the Temple, and on the last day of this feast, he began to speak of rivers of living water. He was claiming that he was the new altar from which living water might flow.

The Festival of Dedication (Hanukkah) occurs next in the year. This is the time commemorating the Lord's deliverance of the people from oppression and rededicating the Temple altar after its desecration. The Jews believed that God's VERY Presence was within the Temple, yet Jesus tells them now that he and the Father are one (*John 10:30*), intimating that the VERY Presence of God is to be found in his Son.

Hanukkah is also called the Festival of Lights, and we had just heard Jesus claiming he was the light of the world. [To learn more about the Jewish holidays, see The Jewish Holidays by Michael Strassfeld, William Morrow, 1985.]

There is another chronology difference in John. In the synoptics, the Last Supper occurs on the first day of Passover (*Matthew 26:17-20; Mark 14:12-17; Luke 22:7-14*), but John tells us Jesus was crucified on the Day of Preparation for the Passover. (*John 19:14*) That was the day when the one-year-old lambs without blemish were prepared for the Passover. (In Exodus, the sacrifice of the lambs had taken place on the eve of the departure.) Jesus, after a one-year ministry encompassing the full annual cycle of festivals, becomes the new Paschal Lamb, the Lamb of God.

In each of these Jewish holidays, John's Gospel has taught that Jesus himself is the embodiment of the holiday's focus.

One can only conclude that John is using his gospel to teach that Jesus brings about a new creation (which is to say a new Genesis); he leads us to the promised land, giving us a new commandment (a new Exodus); he fulfills all the ancient prophecies, illustrating what abundant, eternal life looks like; he replaces the required Jewish festivals and shows where to find God.

John's Gospel puts forth Jesus as the embodiment of the Word of God. After all, it began with that premise: *"And the word became flesh and lived among us."* (*John 1:14*) Even more, Jesus' ministry, as described throughout John, *"is the full disclosure of God in the world, the living sacrament of the kingdom of God."* [Scott Hahn, Consuming the Word, Image, an imprint of the Crown Publishing Group, a division of Random House, NY, 2013, p 100]

The concluding words of the evangelist read, *"These are written so that you may come to believe that Jesus is the Christ, the Son of God, and that through believing you may have life in his name."* (*John 20:31*).

I have in my possession three treasured little books. I have my daughter's copy of "Luther's Small Catechism", which she used to learn the traditions of our faith. I have my own copy of "Luther's Small Catechism", which I had to memorize as a teenager growing up in Luther-land (aka Wisconsin). I have the copy of "Luther's Small Catechism" which both my father and his father before him used when they underwent confirmation.

What did the earliest followers of Jesus use for Christian education? I believe it is possible that John wrote his gospel to be used as a catechism for follows of the Way. Martin Luther's favorite gospel was John. Luther wrote that John "shows us Christ and teaches us everything we need to know."

John is the most creative crucible of Christian education one might imagine. Its twenty chapters reveal to us the entire body of Jewish covenant, tradition, and scripture as we are meant to interpret it—re-aligned through the refracting Light of Jesus. Thanks be to God!

Pondering

How did you first learn about the traditions of your faith?

How did/would you pass these to the next generation?

The Great Marriage Metaphor

There is yet another powerful metaphor pervading the pages of our Bibles. It begins with the covenant bond God established just after he vanquished the Egyptians to deliver the Hebrew people from slavery.

In the Torah

Berit Olam

Moses had led the people to Mt Sinai, where the people are given instructions to prepare to meet their God. All were to wash their clothing and be consecrated for two days, in preparation for the third. (*Exodus 19:10-11*)

"*On the third day*" (a literary marker found throughout the Bible that alerts one that God is about to do something amazing!), there is a theophany of tremendous proportion. There is thunder and lightning, a loud trumpet blast, the mountain wrapped in thick smoke, and violent earth tremors. (*Exodus 19:16-18*) The throng of thousands is approached by God, who enters into a covenant with the people.

A covenant is a binding relationship, like an adoption or marriage. The Jewish perspective is this everlasting covenant (*berit olam* in Hebrew) relationship was as intimate and permanent as a marriage was intended to be. This wedding with the Divine, as it is consecrated, remembered, renewed, recreated, from the pages of Exodus to the concluding chapters of Revelation, is the great marriage metaphor this chapter will explore.

After God's expectations are shared, with the mediation of Moses, (we call these the commandments), there is a blood ceremony to ratify the covenant. (*Exodus 24:4-11*) The wedding vows are exchanged as the people all say, "*All the words that the LORD has spoken we will do.*" (*Exodus 24:3*) Then the wedding "reception" followed: ". . . *they beheld God, and they ate and drank.*" (*Exodus 24:11*)

After this, Moses re-ascends Sinai, where he stays with God for forty days and nights. Think how long forty days lasts—not too much more than a month. Indeed, if your church keeps the liturgical season of Lent, you know precisely the length of time Moses was absent from the camp. Forty days lapsed since thousands of people had an astounding experience of the Very Presence of God, and all of them wholeheartedly vowed this was a *berit olam*—a marriage to last forever.

The people were not easy about Moses' delay, and they became restless, complaining to Moses' brother, Aaron. They begged Aaron to *"make gods for us."* (*Exodus 32:1*) You know the deplorable story; Aaron melts their golden jewelry and casts a molten golden idol of a calf. (*Exodus 32:2-4*) The people proclaim this idol was the god who delivered them from bondage in Egypt. (*Exodus 32:4*)

The next day the people rose early *"and offered burnt offerings and brought sacrifices of well-being; and the people sat down to eat and drink, and rose up to revel."* (*Exodus 32:6*)

Committing idolatry may seem foreign to us, but a closer reading of this text suggests more is going on. The phrase, *"rose up to revel,"* is closer to "rose up to play", and this hints strongly of a pagan practice, common in the ancient Near East, that included cultic prostitution. Idolatry is a type of adultery, when you consider the *berit olam* was a wedding band!

Though an evil precedent had been set, God does move past this episode of idolatry and renews the wedding covenant with Israel. They are given lots of opportunities to obey God's command. Once the people had been led into the land of Canaan, at the hand of Moses' successor Joshua, there is another covenant renewal ceremony.

Joshua gathered all the tribes of Israel. He charges them, *"Now therefore revere the LORD, and serve him in sincerity and faithfulness; put away the gods that your ancestors served beyond the River and in Egypt, and serve the LORD."* (*Joshua 24:14*) Three times, Joshua asks if the people will be faithful. Three times they affirm, *"The LORD our God we will serve, and him we will obey."* (*Joshua 24:24*)

The Runaway Bride

The prophets cannot say enough about this marriage and the subsequent adultery/idolatry. It is an established understanding that God is the divine bridegroom, and Israel is clearly the beloved bride.

"Go and proclaim in the hearing of Jerusalem, Thus says the LORD:
I remember the devotion of your youth, your love as a bride,
how you followed me in the wilderness, in a land not sown." (Jeremiah 2:1-2)

Ezekiel offers an elaborate allegory of God's protection of Israel until she was mature enough to enter the covenantal marriage bond:

"You grew up and became tall and arrived at full womanhood;
. . . I passed by you again and looked on you;
You were at the age for love.
I spread the edge of my cloak over you:
. . . I pledged myself to you and entered into a covenant with you,
Says the Lord GOD, and you became mine." (Ezekiel 16:7-8)

Hosea is a prophet whose own unfaithful wife Gomer serves as an example for God's idolatrous bride. As Hosea takes Gomer back after her adultery, so God will bring his people back to him.

"Therefore, I will now allure her,
and bring her into the wilderness,
and speak tenderly to her.
From there I will give her her vineyards,
and make the Valley of Achor a door of hope.
There she shall respond as in the days of her youth,
as at the time when she came out of the land of Egypt." (Hosea 2:14-15)

The prophets make it very apparent that God's people are as unfaithful as an adulterous wife.

"Can a girl forget her ornaments, or a bride her attire?
Yet my people have forgotten me, days without number." (Jeremiah 2:32)

"How the faithful city has become a whore!
She that was full of justice,
righteousness lodged in her—but now murderers!" (Isaiah 1:21)

"Instead, as a faithless wife leaves her husband,
so you have been faithless to me, O house of Israel, says the LORD." (Jeremiah 3:20)

The faithful bridegroom never gives up on his wayward bride, no matter how much the bride betrays her God in repeated acts of adultery/idolatry. God continues to extend his promises of forgiveness and renewal.

Indeed, the Hebrew Bible is full of God showing his *"hesed"* or steadfast love in every instance.

"And I will take you for my wife forever; I will take you for my wife in righteousness and in justice, in steadfast love, and in mercy. I will take you for my wife in faithfulness; and you shall know the LORD." (Hosea 2:19-20)

"For your Maker is your husband,
the LORD of hosts is his name;
the Holy One of Israel is your Redeemer,
the God of the whole earth he is called.
For the LORD has called you like a wife forsaken and grieved in spirit,
like the wife of a man's youth when she is cast off, says your God.
For a brief moment I abandoned you,
but with great compassion I will gather you.
In overflowing wrath for a moment I hid my face from you,
But with everlasting love I will have compassion on you,
Says the LORD, your Redeemer." (Isaiah 54:5-8)

"The days are surely coming, says the LORD, when I will make a new covenant with the house of Israel and the house of Judah. It will not be like the covenant that I made with their ancestors when I took them by the hand to bring them out of the land of Egypt—a covenant that they broke, though I was their husband, says the LORD. But this is the covenant that I will make with the house of Israel after those days, says the LORD: I will put my law within them, and I will write it on their hearts; and I will be their God, and they shall be my people." (Jeremiah 31:31-33)

"Thus says the LORD: In this place of which you say, 'It is a waste without human beings or animals, in the towns of Judah and the streets of Jerusalem that are desolate, without inhabitants, human or animal, there shall once more be heard the voice of mirth and the voice of gladness, the voice of the bridegroom and the voice of the bride, the voices of those who sing, as they bring thank offerings to the house of the LORD:
'Give thanks to the LORD of hosts,
for the LORD is good,
for his steadfast love endures forever!'" (Jeremiah 33:10-11)

A beautiful image in this passage is that the voices will be of joy. We will hear an echo of this joy again in the gospel according to John.

All the examples stress an important point. God's forgiveness is not only about forgiveness of sin. The goal is reunion with God. The bridegroom wants the bride to be in a faithful, eternal marriage.

Erotic Love Poem

As explained in the earlier essay on the vine metaphor, the Song of Solomon is interpreted as an allegory for the bridegroom God's love for the bride Israel. It is interesting that there are several examples of shared words between the Song of Solomon and the "*Shema*". The *Shema* is an extremely well-known passage from Deuteronomy, which is prayed three times daily by observant Jews:

"Hear, O Israel: The LORD is our God, the LORD alone. You shall love the LORD your God with all your heart, and with all your soul, and with all your might." (Deuteronomy 6:4-5)

The phrase, *"whom my soul loves"* is repeated in Song of Solomon *1:7; 3:1; 3:2; 3:3;* and *3:4.* This shared phrase is evidence that God is, indeed, the bridegroom in the love poem.

The speech of the bridegroom is desirable and sweet, as found in Song of Solomon and Psalm 19:

"His speech is most sweet, and he is altogether desirable.
This is my beloved and this is my friend, O daughters of Jerusalem." (Song of Solomon 5:16)

"The fear of the LORD is pure, enduring forever;
the ordinances of the LORD are true and righteous altogether.
More to be desired are they than gold, even much fine gold;
sweeter also than honey, and the drippings of the honeycomb." (Psalm 19:9-10)

The bride refers to the bridegroom as a shepherd, while Psalm 23 refers to God also as a shepherd:

"Tell me, you whom my soul loves, where you pasture your flock,
where you make it lie down at noon." (Song of Solomon 1:7)

"The LORD is my shepherd, I shall not want.
He makes me lie down in green pastures." (Psalm 23:1-2)

There are enough comparisons to affirm the identification of the LORD as the beloved in the Song of Solomon.

Author Brant Pitre, in his book <u>Jesus the Bridegroom</u> [Image, 2018], addresses in detail the many Biblical passages that bring forth these comparisons. Interestingly, he also records ample passages from the Song of Solomon as compared to certain of the historic books of the Old Testament (2 Chronicles and 1 Kings, for example) to make the case that the bride is described in similar terms as was the Temple in Jerusalem.

It is a surprise, then, when the erotic love poem, Song of Solomon, does not end with a wedding. Instead, it ends with the bride waiting for the bridegroom to *"make haste"* to join her. (*Song of Solomon 8:14*)

The Song of Solomon is the last book in The Writings, or the Kethuvim, of the Tanakh. So, it is appropriate to proceed now to the New Testament gospel accounts with their references to weddings.

Wedding Rituals

The inaugural act of Jesus' public ministry takes place at a wedding, a wedding that takes place "on the third day" (a literary marker to look for something amazing to happen!). Jesus and his mother Mary are attending a wedding in the town of Cana (a name that coincidentally means "daughter-in-law"). Read the whole account in John 2:1-10. It is helpful to know something about Jewish wedding celebrations in the first century AD. They lasted an entire week; that is, seven days of feasting and joyful celebration. (*Judges 14:17*)

It was the responsibility of the bridegroom to keep the food and wine flowing. If you have ever been involved in the planning of a wedding, you know how much planning and preparation is involved to be sure there is food and drink to satisfy people for just a couple of hours at a wedding reception. Can you imagine the responsibility lasting for seven days?

A Jewish person who heard Mary say to Jesus, "*they have no wine*," (*John 2:3*) might hear an echo of an Isaiah passage:

"*The wine dries up, the vine languishes,*
all the merry-hearted sigh.
The mirth of the timbrels is stilled,
the noise of the jubilant has ceased,
the mirth of the lyre is stilled.
No longer do they drink wine with singing." (*Isaiah 24:7-9*)

Anyone who recognized this prophetic passage would also know what text follows, and it is a description of what would come to be called "The Messianic Banquet".

"*On this mountain the LORD of hosts will make for all peoples*
a feast of rich food, a feast of well-aged wines,

of rich food filled with marrow, of well-aged wines strained clear.
And he will destroy on this mountain
the shroud that is cast over all peoples,
the sheet that is spread over all nations;
He will swallow up death forever." (Isaiah 25:6-8)

In the story of the wedding at Cana, Jesus does change the water into wine, in the first sign of the glory of God recorded in John. The remarkable thing is the amount of wine produced. The stone jars were for water used in Jewish purification rites, so they were large enough to hold 20 or 30 gallons each. That means, with six jars, approximately 120 to 180 gallons of wine would be provided. Now, that's a party! The extravagance of this much wine would also perhaps recall prophetic passages from the prophets Amos and Joel, passages that spoke of a future age of salvation anticipated by the Jews.

"In that day the mountains shall drip sweet wine,
the hills shall flow with milk,
and all the stream beds of Judah
shall flow with water;
a fountain shall come forth from the house of the LORD." (Joel 3:18)

The "Messianic Banquet", for Christians, may culminate the vision of the wedding being described by John of Patmos in Revelation 21, but it is founded upon a Jewish view "of the *olam ha-ba*, the 'world to come'" that included "a banquet, a great feast at which one reclined at table with Abraham, Isaac, and Jacob." [Amy-Jill Levine, Short Stories by Jesus, Harper Collins Publishing, 2014, p 13] See Matthew 8:11 for a hint of this.

Soon after the wedding at Cana, evangelist John offers another unique story, a tale of Jesus' encounter with a Samaritan woman at a well. It is possible that a meeting at a well is another literary device in the Bible. Can you remember some other examples of women being met at wells? Rebekah, who will become the wife of patriarch Isaac, is found at a well. (*Genesis 24:15-16*) Patriarch Jacob will meet his future wife Rachel at a well. (*Genesis 29:1-9*) Moses, also, meets his future wife Zipporah at a well. (*Exodus 2:15-17, 21*) In all three cases, the women are "foreign".

When Jesus encounters a foreign woman at well, first-century Jewish ears are conditioned to expect this Samaritan woman might be a potential bride! That certainly explains the disciples shock at learning of this encounter. (*John 4:27*)

Author Brant Pitre, in <u>Jesus the Bridegroom</u>, ponders this account with some detail. The Samaritan woman has had multiple husbands already. The Samaritans worshipped idols called "the Baals", which is a Canaanite word for "husbands"! The Samaritan woman mentions the well of Jacob. That well, according to Jewish tradition, was a flowing spring. Water that is flowing is considered "living" water, as opposed to water that stands still as in a cistern or puddle. Living water supports life. Custom dictated that a Jewish bride have a ritual bath in living water prior to her marriage ceremony. If you wish to read more of these amazing parallels, do seek the Pitre text.

We do know that a wedding then and now would have had a best man to support the bridegroom. Evangelist John identifies Jesus' cousin, John, who will be called the Baptist, as the best man:

"You yourselves are my witnesses that I said, 'I am not the Messiah, but I have been sent ahead of him.' He who has the bride is the bridegroom. The friend of the bridegroom, who stands and hears him, rejoices greatly at the bridegroom's voice. For this reason my joy has been fulfilled." (John 3:28-29)

This quotation attributed to John the Baptist, obviously recalls the Jeremiah 33 passage quoted earlier, about the voice of the bridegroom and the coming of joy.

We know the friend of the bridegroom, the best man, was a public witness to the wedding. It was also his job to lead the bride to the bridegroom at the proper time for the ceremony. One could consider the activities of John the Baptist as doing that, as he called the people of Israel to repentance in preparation for the coming of the Messiah.

A Memorable Wedding Banquet

Evangelist Matthew tells a parable about a wedding banquet given by a king for his son. Those who like to allegorize parables instantly suspect the king is God and the son is Jesus. When all was ready, with the oxen and calves prepared for the feast, the invitees found better things to do. Some even scoffed at the couriers sent to remind them of the banquet and others mistreated and murdered the messengers. This enraged the king, as you might imagine. Since the banquet was standing ready, everyone in the streets was invited to fill the banquet hall. Did things turn out happily ever after?

In a surprising conclusion, one of the newly invited guests did not have on a *"wedding robe"*! The king commands he be bound and thrown *"into the outer darkness."* (*Matthew 22:1-14*)

The problem is, does it fit that God is an angry king? I think not. We must always try to hear Jesus as a first century Jew might have done. An author who helps with this is Amy-Jill Levine in her book Short Stories by Jesus: The Enigmatic Parables of a Controversial Rabbi [HarperOne, 2014]. One thing a first century Jew would have had would be a better knowledge of the Hebrew Bible than most of us have.

There is actually a story with several parallels in 2 Chronicles 30:1-26 about an invitation extended by King Hezekiah for all Israel and Judah to attend a Passover meal. He obviously wishes for a reunification of the northern and southern tribes.

Those messengers sent to the northern tribes were scorned, and the northern tribes did not attend. Everyone else attended the memorable feasting that was to last seven days, just as a wedding feast would have done.

We learn from first-century historian Josephus that when Assyria conquered Samaria in 722 BC/BCE, it was a result of their refusal to accept King Hezekiah's invitation. Those ten northern tribes are lost forever and sent into outer darkness (Assyrian exile); much *"weeping and gnashing of teeth"* occurred. (*Matthew 22:13*)

So, perhaps rather than just a parable, this story in Matthew is a sample of apocalyptic writing. In apocalyptic literature, the author, living during a time of challenge, takes an event from the past and rewrites it as something yet to happen in the future, in an effort to warn the current audience of a danger. Could Matthew be suggesting his audience not disregard the king's/God's/the bridegroom's invitation, because they might not want to end up like the "lost tribes" of the north? Their casting out was perhaps not punishment so much as a result of their lack of unification with their whole family (all twelve tribes together).

But, what about the lack of a wedding robe in Matthew's story? Again, knowledge of the Hebrew Bible could help:

"I will greatly rejoice in the LORD,
my whole being shall exult in my God;
for he has clothed me with the garments of salvation,
he has covered me with the robe of righteousness,
as a bridegroom decks himself with a garland,
and as a bride adorns herself with her jewels." (Isaiah 61:10)

Weaving together all these scriptural threads, we can see that Matthew, Jesus, and Hezekiah all hope people will respond to God's extravagant invitation to the banquet, to a renewal of the marriage vows.

A Bride Adorned

From the Torah, the Nevi'im, the Kethuvim, and the Gospels, we have been reminded again and again that God's covenant commitment is as intimate and life-giving as a faithful marriage relationship. Our Bibles close with the marriage of God and humanity.

"Then I saw a new heaven and a new earth; for the first heaven and the first earth had passed away, and the sea was no more. And I saw the holy city, the new Jerusalem, coming down out of heaven from God, prepared as a bride adorned for her husband. And I heard a loud voice from the throne saying,
'See the home of God is among mortals.
He will dwell with them;
they will be his peoples,
and God himself will be with them;
he will wipe every tear from their eyes.
Death will be no more;
Mourning and crying and pain will be no more,
For the first things have passed away." (Revelation 21:1-4)

The bride is described in the rest of chapter 21. The bride is the New Jerusalem. And, this exactly fulfills our Old Testament prophecy:

"For Zion's sake I will not keep silent,
And for Jerusalem's sake I will not rest . . .
You shall be a crown of beauty in the hand of the LORD,
And a royal diadem in the hand of your God.
You shall no more be termed Forsaken,
And your land shall no more be termed Desolate;
But you shall be called My Delight Is in Her,
And your land Married;
For the LORD delights in you,
And your land shall be married." (Isaiah 62:1, 3-5)

The wedding supper is ready . . . open your invitation!

Appendix One
A Very Short Summary of the Bible

Hebrew Bible (Old Testament)

Genesis—tales of creation, Noah & flood, and the patriarchal history of Abraham's family

Exodus—Moses leads Israelites out of bondage in Egypt to Mt Sinai; God's covenant commands; forty years wandering in wilderness

Leviticus—legal codes

Numbers—Moses' leadership continues during the wilderness sojourn

Deuteronomy—retelling the story of Moses

Joshua—conquest of Canaan

Judges—period of time before monarchy when local leaders ruled

Ruth—faithful foreigner becomes great grandmother of King David

1 & 2 Samuel—man of God named Samuel anoints first two kings, Saul then David

1 & 2 Kings—King Solomon builds the Temple; subsequent kings of Israel and Judah, the divided kingdom; the prophet Elijah

1 & 2 Chronicles—retelling of history of kings, ending with fall of Jerusalem

Ezra & Nehemiah—return after the exile in Babylon, rebuilding the Temple

Esther—Hebrew queen in Persia saves her people (origin of Purim)

Job—man who suffers great hardships questions God's justice

Psalms—collection of liturgical songs

Proverbs—pithy sayings about life

Ecclesiastes—musings about life

Song of Solomon—love poem

Isaiah—prophetic writings of exhortation and encouragement, and Messianic texts

Jeremiah & Lamentations—prophetic writings of exhortation and encouragement

Ezekiel—while in exile, Ezekiel envisions God's return to Temple

Daniel—apocalyptic vision—keep the faith while in exile

Hosea, Joel, Amos, Obadiah, Jonah, Micah, Nahum, Habakkuk, Zephaniah,

Haggai, Zechariah, Malachi—twelve minor scrolls with words of prophets from before, during, and after the exile

New Testament

Matthew, Mark, Luke—gospel accounts of the ministry and passion story of Jesus

John—gospel with a different focus on the ministry and passion of Jesus

Acts of the Apostles—sequel by Luke telling stories of Peter and Paul

Romans, 1 & 2 Corinthians, Galatians, Ephesians, Philippians, Colossians,

1 & 2 Thessalonians, 1 & 2 Timothy, Titus, Philemon, Hebrews,

James, 1 & 2 Peter, 1,2,3 John, Jude—various epistles, many credited to missionary apostle Paul

Revelation—apocalyptic vision cycles by John of Patmos asking, *"Whom do you worship?"*

Appendix Two
Number Symbolism in the Bible

3

Three (3) stands for the divinity:

+Trinity (Triune God = Father, Son, and Holy Spirit)

+Past, present, and future tenses in the name of YHWH (Exodus 3)

+Three facets of *Shema* (Deuteronomy 6:5)—"You shall love the LORD your God with all your heart, and with all your soul, and with all your might."

+Three gifts of the Magi (Matthew 2:11)

+Three annual festivals requiring pilgrimages to Jerusalem for all able-bodied males (Exodus 23:14)

+"On the third day," used 36 times in Old Testament and 17 times in the New Testament, signifies God is about to do something new (i.e. Genesis 22:4; Genesis 42:18; Exodus 19:11; 2 Samuel 1:2; Hosea 6:2; John 2:1; Acts 9:9)

4

Four (4) represents earthly or created things:

+Four seasons

+Four cardinal directions/four corners of the earth/four winds

+Four rivers watered the garden of Eden (Genesis 2:10-14)

+Four phases of the moon each month

+Four elements, according to the ancient understanding: earth, water, fire, and air

+Four "living" creatures described in both Ezekiel and Revelation

+Four "horsemen" in the books of Zechariah and Revelation

7

Seven (7), as obtained by adding the divine number (3) to the earthly number (4), represents completion or perfection:

+Seven days for God to complete creation

+Seventh day is hallowed (Sabbath)

+Sabbatical rest every seventh year for the land (Leviticus 25:3-4)

+Jubilee year proclaimed after 7 weeks times 7 years (Leviticus 25:8-12)

+Joseph's dreams (Genesis 37) involved sets of seven items

+Job was blessed with seven sons (Job 1:2; 42:13)

+Seven loaves of fishes were multiplied by Jesus (Matthew 15:36)

+Seven baskets of food remained after the multitude was fed (Matthew 15:37)

+Passover lasts seven days

+The Jewish period of mourning (*Shiv'ah*) is seven days

+Roman Catholics have seven deadly sins, seven heavenly virtues, and seven sacraments

+There are serious series of sevens in Revelation, including seven churches, seven stars, seven thunders, seven plagues, seven spirits, seven seals on scrolls, seven angels with trumpets, seven golden bowls, seven golden lampstands, seven diadems, seven mountains, seven beatitudes, and several seven-fold listings in the seven vision cycles!

8

Eight (8), as one more than the complete number seven (7), suggests continuance and hope:

+Eight human souls survived on Noah's ark during the flood of forty days and forty nights (Genesis 7:7)

+Hanukkah, the festival of light and rededication of the Temple lasts for eight days

+Males were circumcised on the 8th day (Genesis 17:12; Genesis 21:4; Luke 2:21)

10

Ten (10), which is obtained by adding the divine number (3) to the complete number (7), stands for human completeness:

+Ten fingers

+Ten toes

+Basis of the decimal system

+Basis of the metric system

+Ten commandments (although these are not actually numbered in Exodus, nor do the different denominations identify the same ten!)

+Ten talents in Matthew's parable

+Ten bridesmaids in Matthew's parable

+Ten lepers healed by Jesus

12

Twelve (12), obtained by multiplying the divine number (3) by the earthly number (4), represents organized religion:

+Twelve tribes of Israel in the Hebrew Bible

+Twelve disciples of Jesus in the New Testament

+Twelve remaining baskets of food, after Jesus fed the multitude (Luke 9:17)

+Twelve kinds of fruit on the tree of life (Revelation 22:2)

+Twelve pearl gates on the holy city of New Jerusalem (Revelation 21:12)

+Other religious systems use 12: twelve signs of the Zodiac; twelve Greek deities lived atop Mt Olympos; Arthurian legend assigned twelve knights placement at the Round Table

40

Forty (40), obtained by multiplying the earthly number (4) by the number for human completeness (10), suggests a full dimension of human suffering or endurance:

+Flood experienced by Noah began with forty days and forty nights of rain

+Joseph's physicians in Egypt required forty days to embalm patriarch Jacob upon his death

+Israel's sojourn in the wilderness lasted forty years

+Moses was atop Mt Sinai forty days

+Spies were sent into Canaan by Moses for forty days

+Elijah was in the wilderness forty days

+Jonah prophesied that Nineveh would be overturned in forty days

+Jesus fasted in the wilderness forty days

+There are forty days between Jesus' resurrection and the ascension

+The liturgical season of Lent lasts forty days

70

Seventy (70), which is obtained by multiplying the number of human completeness (10) by the perfect number (7), represents a full dimension of human completeness:

+There were seventy people in the household of Jacob entering Egypt (Genesis 46:27)

+The table of nations (Genesis 10:1) totals seventy

+Number of years allotted to a human lifespan (Psalm 90:10)

+A length of exile and the time before forgiveness (Daniel 9:2,24; Jeremiah 25:11,12; Jeremiah 29:10)

+Number of elders who aided Moses with leadership (Numbers 11:24-25)

+Organization of followers sent out by Jesus (Luke 10:1-6)

+Seventy times seven for the extent of forgiveness (Matthew 18:21-22)

6

Six (6) as one less than or short of the perfect number (7), indicates imperfection:

+Sometimes this is intensified as in "666". So, if God is addressed as "Holy, Holy, Holy", then recognizing that the highest evil is "Unholy, Unholy, Unholy", 666 emphasizes this imperfection

3 ½

Since it is half of the perfect number (7), this number suggests the limited supremacy of evil. It will take a bit of calculating to discover it in the Bible:

+Both Daniel 7:25 and 12:7 refer to "a time, two times, and half time", with "time" actually standing for the word "year". Thus, the verses are suggesting 3 ½ years.

+The "forty-two months" mentioned in Revelation 11:2 can be understood as 3 ½ years.

+The "one thousand two hundred sixty days" mentioned in Revelation 12:6 may be understood as 3 ½ years.

+Revelation 11:11 mentions "three and a half days"

144

As the product of 12 x 12 (the number of organized religion), 144 indicates the peak of organization:

+The wall of the New Jerusalem in Revelation 21:17 is 144 cubits

1000

One thousand (1000) is the product of 10 x 10 x 10, or 10³, and therefore it is the most perfect number:

+"With the Lord one day is like a thousand years, and a thousand years are like one day." (2 Peter 3:8)

+The dragon in Revelation 20:2 is bound for 1000 years

+The martyrs in Revelation 20:4 reign with Christ for 1000 years

+Also, the shape of a cube (10³) is considered to be perfection.

+In Ezekiel's 47th chapter, the measurement of the temple is described as 1000 cubits square

+In 1 Kings 6:20, the dimension for the Holy of Holies within Solomon's Temple forms a perfect cube

+The holy city in Revelation 21 is described as a perfect cube

144,000

144,000 represents the ultimate totality. It is obtained by multiplying several excellent numbers: 12 x 12 x 1000.

The concept of a million was not really developed prior to the Middle Ages, so when 144,000 is encountered in Revelation 7:4 or 14:3, it is just the largest number possible. In other words, no one is left behind!

Appendix Three
Literary Forms of the Bible

Some vocabulary will assist you in parsing the types of writing within the Biblical texts. First, there are many categories in literature, from autobiography, to historical fiction, to myth, to debate, to romance novel, to name a few. These differing categories are called *genres*. Our Bible, being a collection of sixty-six distinct books, covers just about any genre you might imagine, including legal codes, epistles, and sermons.

Within any genre that an author elects to use for his writing, there are different choices for the *literary form* that is used in the work. Examples might be prose or poetry, apocalypse, parable or allegory.

There are also "smaller" *literary devices* used by authors to express themselves. You probably remember learning about similes and metaphors in high school English class. These are comparisons between things, with a simile adding the words "like" or "as", i.e. he runs like the wind, and metaphors being a straight comparison, i.e. she is an absolute angel.

The metaphors used in John's Gospel are such comparisons, used to give us glimpses into the mysteries of the Divine which are beyond our limited human understanding. Lutheran theologian and author Barbara Rossing [The Rapture Exposed, Westview Press, 2004] explores the extensive metaphor found in Revelation of the "Lamb". Of course, a person is not a lamb, but our understanding of lamb-ness and the historical understanding of Passover and sacrificial lambs, adds layers of insight into recognizing Jesus as the Paschal Lamb.

You are undoubtedly familiar with one of Jesus' preferred teaching styles, which is the telling of parables. A parable is a teaching story that juxtaposes everyday things (such as seeds) with things of the Divine (such as the kingdom or reign of God). The parable will have a comparison that calls attention to our preconceived ideas and suggests a fresh perspective to them.

Some parables give a simple example. Some parables are enacted, which is to say that the message is the action itself. Parables are always meant as a challenge, inviting the audience to reflect, react, and respond.

It has been a tendency for Christians to turn parables into allegories. An allegory has layers of meaning that sometimes change the historical and social context of the parable. That means the original audience would not have perceived the same moral of the story. An excellent example of this is St Augustine's (a fourth-century theologian) approaching the Good Samaritan parable as allegory. He suggested the man going down to Jericho was Adam. The wounds afflicted were his sins. The priest and the Levite were the Old Testament. The Samaritan was Jesus, who bound up his wounds/sins. [For more on this explanation, see Margaret Nutting Ralph, And God Said What?, Paulist Press, 2003]

Augustine's explanation shows ingenuity, which makes it appealing to many, but is this the lesson Jesus was teaching his audience? Of course, Jesus' original audience could not have figured this out! It is most helpful to listen to the parables as the original audiences would have heard them. "Jesus told parables, not allegories." [Amy-Jill Levine, Short Stories of Jesus, Harper Collins, 2014]

This summary is just a hint of the rich literary forms used by many authors over hundreds of years whose words have found their way into our Bibles.

Printed in the United States
By Bookmasters